PROFIT FOR THE POOR

Cases in Micro-Finance

PROFIT FOR THE POOR

Cases in Micro-Finance

Malcolm Harper

PUBLISHING

Published by ITDG Publishing
103-105 Southampton Row, London WC1B 4HL, UK
www.itdgpublishing.org.uk

© Malcolm Harper 1998

First published in 1998
Reprinted 2001

ISBN 1 85339 438 6

All rights reserved. No part of this publication may be reprinted or reproduced or utilized in any form or by any electronic, mechanical, or other means, now known or hereafter invented, including photocopying and recording, or in any information storage or retrieval system, without the written permission of the publishers.

A catalogue record for this book is available from the British Library.

ITDG Publishing is the publishing arm of the Intermediate Technology Development Group. Our mission is to build the skills and capacity of people in developing countries through the dissemination of information in all forms, enabling them to improve the quality of their lives and that of future generations.

Printed in India

ACKNOWLEDGEMENTS

None of the case studies in this book were written without some assistance from other people. A number of them include a note of acknowledgement to those who helped to put them together, or who actually wrote them. I thank them again.

There are many other people, however, whose names do not appear, partly because I do not know them all, and partly because there are too many of them. These are the staff of the institutions, at all levels, and particularly junior staff who so often have insights which their seniors lack, but above all they are the clients. The cases attempt to look at micro-finance from their point of view, and they are the people who most deserve to be acknowledged. Some of their names appear in the case studies, but it is doubtful if they will ever read the book. They have better things to do, and better ways of spending their money, and many of them cannot read in English or any other language. Most are not named, but their anonymous assistance is nevertheless gratefully acknowledged.

I never cease to be astonished at the willingness of ordinary people to share what I should consider private information about their debts, their assets, their businesses and their incomes. Not all the information is accurate, although I suspect that little of it is deliberately mis-stated, and some people may cooperate in anticipation of preferential treatment. Most people, I believe, cooperate with a prying stranger because they are polite and helpful by nature, and they may too be pleased that someone is interested in the details of their lives. I wonder, however, how I myself would respond to questions of the kind I unhesitatingly put to others.

In addition to the institutions whose operations are described, I must also thank three others whose generosity has given me the time, and the facilities, to put together this collection. Cranfield University School of Management allowed me to work in this, to them quite foreign, field for 21 years; the Director, Professor Leo Murray, has never failed to facilitate my efforts. Father Michael Bogaert S.J. erstwhile Director of Xavier Institute of Management, in Bhubaneswar, first showed me how micro-enterprise could help to alleviate poverty in India.

The Ford Foundation has generously supported and gently steered my work for many years. Many of its staff have tolerated my eccentricities over this period, but I should like particularly to thank Jane Rosser of the New Delhi office for all her help.

MALCOLM HARPER

CONTENTS

Acknowledgements   v

Section 1: Introduction and Some General Issues

Chapter 1. Introduction	3
Chapter 2. Interest Rates	11
Chapter 3. Where is the Money to Come From?	18
Chapter 4. The Institutions	23

Section 2: Case Studies

Chapter 5. The Bhawal Rajbari Branch, Grameen Bank, Bangladesh	33
Chapter 6. The Banco Nacional de Comercio Interior, Mexico	45
Chapter 7. The Gazaria Branch, BRAC, Bangladesh	52
Chapter 8. The Omdurman Productive Families Branch of the Sudan-Islamic Bank	60
Chapter 9. The Laxmi Mahila Sangam and Myrada, Karnataka State, India	69
Chapter 10. PRIDE and KREP, Two Examples from Machakos, Kenya	75
Chapter 11. The Kenya Industrial Estates Informal Sector Programme, Murang'a Branch	90
Chapter 12. Cuttack Urban Cooperative Bank—College Square Branch	99
Chapter 13. Masoko Madogo Madogo Market Society, Dar Es Salaam, Tanzania	106
Chapter 14. The Pingua Branch of the Dhenkanal Gramya Bank, Orissa, India: 'Linkage' to Self Help Groups	115
Chapter 15. Puri Gramin Bank and DSS Balipatna, Orissa, India	124
Chapter 16. Bank Rakyat Indonesia — Contoh Unit	132
Chapter 17. The Start-Up Fund, South Africa	141
Chapter 18. The Kalanjiam Community Banking System, Madurai East, Tamil Nadu, India	148
Chapter 19. Basix Finance, Raichur, Karnataka, India	162

Section 3: Conclusions

Chapter 20. Conclusions   175

Section 1

INTRODUCTION AND SOME GENERAL ISSUES

CHAPTER 1

INTRODUCTION

What is This Book for ?

Micro-finance is fashionable, and like any development fashion it is celebrated as much in print as in reality. Any writer of a new book should therefore accept that the onus of proof is on him; is yet another book justified ?

One objective of this book is to show that there are many different ways of 'skinning the cat'; that is, of bringing sustainable financial services to poor people. Some of the institutions and the systems they operate are very well known and have had books written about them already, while others are small and obscure. None of them is perfect, and none is a blueprint for any situation other than the one where it evolved. All of them, however, have successfully brought financial services to people who would not otherwise have had access to them.

The cases are not representative of the whole field; there are many different approaches to micro-finance, and many countries where the new 'industry' is well-developed, which are omitted. The examples were chosen because they seemed interesting and because the writer had an opportunity to spend time at the actual branches and with their clients. The wide range, of the institutions and of their methods, gives a flavour of the diversity that characterises the whole endeavour; if the collection dispels any illusion that there is one 'right way', it will have served its purpose.

The material for the case studies has been gathered over a period of about seven years, so that some of the figures are out-of-date, and the scale, the standards and the methods of many of the institutions have changed a great deal since the cases were written. It is perhaps premature to talk of the 'history' of modern micro-finance, but readers who are personally familiar with some of the institutions may learn something of the pace of recent change.

All the cases, however, have lessons which are relevant today. Most of them have been used as training material in courses for people who work in or fund micro-finance, and some of those who learned (or suffered) in those courses are now employed by the institutions which are described.

There are also large numbers of institutions which have not reached the stage which some of the older cases in this book describe. In some sense, the wheel does have to be re-invented, and this book may shed some light on the process as well as showing how some steps can possibly be shortened.

Over a third of the cases are from India, and four are from the State of Orissa. India has the dubious distinction of having more absolutely poor people than have ever lived in any one country, and Orissa is one of the poorest states of India. The poor are the customers of micro-finance, so India must be the biggest potential market.

The Indian experience in micro-finance has also been somewhat neglected, perhaps because it has been overshadowed by the long and generally unsuccessful history of government sponsored poverty alleviation programmes. As some of the cases in this book show, India does have a great deal to teach others in this field.

The main body of the book consists of fifteen case studies, each of which describes one system, (except the case from Machakos in Kenya which compares two systems) and, to a limited extent, the institution which operates it. The case studies are not written, however, from the point of view of the systems or the institutions as such. They attempt to describe the ways in which their customers, members, clients or beneficiaries were able to use them. It is hoped that readers will get some understanding of what it is like to be a customer of each institution, and what difference it has made to their lives.

All the case studies also include financial information, usually in the form of simple accounts for the financial institutions, generally at the branch level. These show the income and expenditure of the banking operation, and there are also simple balance sheets to show how the money is being used, and where it has come from. These accounts have been very much simplified, and in some cases they were put together for the purposes of the case study, since the organisation did not have up to date information of this sort. They do show, however, the degree to which the institutions are self-sustaining, however that term may be defined, and it is usually possible to make a rough estimate of the amount of subsidy that the institution is receiving, if it is.

In some cases foreign exchange values have changed very significantly since the financial information was obtained, and official exchange rates do not always reflect the costs of living. For the purposes of understanding the economics of the various financial systems, however, the relationships between figures are in many respects more important than the absolute values. The foreign exchange rates against the US dollar are given for background information rather than for precise calculations.

Most of the cases also include simple financial data for some of the customers, which show the extent to which they are benefiting, in economic terms. The reader should not assume that micro-finance institutions can be judged purely in financial terms, but banking is about money, and unless they can pay for themselves the institutions will be permanently dependent on outside assistance. This is presumably not what their customers, their managers or most readers of this book would want.

The cases can be read like chapters in a book, by individual readers who wish to have a general overview of the subject, and to learn something about the range of different ways in which micro-finance can be delivered. They can also be used singly or in combination in training courses on development finance. It would obviously be much better actually to visit the programmes and to talk with their customers, but the written cases can at least give an impression of what is being done.

Each case is followed by some questions which may suggest lines of thought to the individual reader and which can also be used as a basis for class discussion. Some comments are also included, but neither they nor the questions should be treated as exhaustive; every reader, and every training group, will discover new ideas and new insights. It should be stressed that the comments and questions are designed to provoke and even to irritate; the writer by no means always shares the points of view that are implied, but they merit consideration.

The case studies are preceded by separate chapters on the origins of micro-finance, on interest rates and sources of finance, and on some institutional issues. There are of course many more topics which could also have been covered, such as gender and empowerment, management information systems, staff recruitment, training and motivation and the role of foreign donors. Some if not all of these emerge naturally from consideration of the case studies, and others have already been exhaustively covered elsewhere. The case studies can speak for themselves.

Is Micro-finance New ?

The book is about profitable micro-finance. The case studies describe a variety of different ways by which it is possible to provide financial services to poor people at a price which they can afford, and which also covers the costs of the institution.

Not all the groups and institutions, or their branches which are described in the case studies, were profitable when the case studies were written, and some of them might prefer to be judged by the less specific but more fashionable standards of 'sustainability'. Most of those which are not covering all their costs now, however, do have the potential to make profits in the future.

Micro-finance has been described as a 'new world', but if it can be genuinely profitable, why is it that this business opportunity has for so long gone unrecognised ? In fact, of course, it is not a new world at all, any more than the Americas were new when they were 'discovered' in 1492. They were only new to Columbus, and to the people of the 'old world', but they had been there all the time, and were well known to the people who lived there.

Poor people have always had their own traditional financial systems, which both exploit them and serve them. What is new is that people in 'modern' formal financial institutions, which have evolved to serve the financial needs of the rich, are beginning to recognise that they can learn from the informal financial intermediaries that serve the poor, and that there may even be profits to be made in this 'new' market, which is really the oldest financial marketplace of all. Financial services used to be regarded as a form of assistance to small enterprises; now they are coming to be seen as another type of enterprise themselves.

'Modern' micro-finance such as is described in these case studies owes its origins to two long-standing but very different institutions, the moneylender and the local savings group. Moneylenders, like middlemen in general, have traditionally been despised and demolished. Jesus Christ is said to have overthrown their tables in front of the temple in Jerusalem over two thousand years ago, and Shakespeare's Shylock is only one of many classic moneylender villains.

Local savings groups have never been hated, but have until recently been disregarded by formal financial institutions, except possibly as a form of deposit mobilisation. Nearly every society in the world has some traditional form of regular savings mechanism, with or without a credit component, but they have been seen as the poor man's, or more usually poor woman's, substitute for formal banking, not as a potentially profitable distribution channel for banking services.

The success of the micro-finance institutions which are described in these case studies, however, is in large measure due to their adoption of many of the strengths of these two traditional forms of financial intermediation. Their future will depend on how successfully they continue to match the merits of the older systems and at the same time overcome their disadvantages.

Moneylenders

Market imperfections such as poor communications often allow moneylenders to impose local monopolies, and the very small local scale of their operations means that they have to charge what appear to be high rates of interest on the limited funds they have to lend. These rates may be even higher because moneylending is in theory illegal in many places, so a premium has to be added to cover the cost of illegality and the impossibility of pursuing debts through the courts. Millions of poor people in South Asia are still indebted to local moneylenders, and these debts are often passed down from generation to generation; the loans may be serviced by bonded labour, but the principal is never repaid, and the moneylender is happy for it to remain that way.

Moneylenders are however themselves micro-entrepreneurs, and like any other business their survival depends on their ability to satisfy the needs of their customers. They offer fast, convenient and informal service, repayments can be flexible, and they are willing to lend for so-called 'consumption' as well as 'productive' purposes. Unlike many bankers, they are aware that their customers need to spend money on food, education, house repairs, health care and clothing in order to be able to earn money, so they are willing to make loans for these purposes as well as for business and farming. They realise that the distinction is largely meaningless.

There are also many modern variants of traditional moneylenders, whose businesses owe nothing to the recent innovations in micro-finance. Pawnbrokers enable poor people to make use of what few assets they have to mobilise funds when they need them, and goldsmiths not only sell jewellery but also offer an 'after-sales service' by lending money on the security of what they have sold. In Indonesia and elsewhere village goldsmiths recognise the certificates of authenticity which others have provided; they advance money up to the value of the gold contained in jewellery, and allow borrowers to recover the items on repayment plus a fee. Before 1971, when the price of gold was fixed in dollars by an international agreement, investment in this form provided poor people with an instantly convertible form of savings with at least some element of inflation protection.

Savings and Credit Groups

There are almost as many names for local savings groups as there are languages. In English they are also called rotating savings and credit associations (ROSCAs), chit funds and merry-go-rounds, and their methods of operation differ widely. Like moneylenders, they too share certain advantages, which have enabled them to survive and grow, in rich and poor communities, in spite of competition from formal financial institutions.

They are above all familiar; the local moneylender is usually a near neighbour, which is one of his strengths, but he (or often she, the term 'middleman' has not been gender-sensitised, but there are probably as many local female moneylenders as there are men) is generally richer and may not be from the same community in a caste or socio-economic sense. The members of local savings groups, however, are usually not only neighbours but are also friends and fellow workers. The savings group provides what is often the only opportunity for social interaction, particularly for women in some communities. The regular obligation to save may be no more than the 'glue' which brings the group together and holds it together, providing a base for other more important activities.

These groups are always handicapped, however, by the same features which give them their strength. They are started, financed and managed by the same small local group of people whom they serve, and their financial resources are limited by the ability of these people to save, and to generate additional funds from the profits they earn by investing their savings.

In many cases, their opportunities for profitable investment are limited by social restrictions, the lack of markets and their lack of skills and ignorance of whatever few opportunities which may be available. There are many such groups which have accumulated quite large sums, even over many years, and have made little or no use of them. The confidence which the members of these groups gain from having saved money regularly, and having control over it, may be more valuable than any use they could actually make of it. People in this situation cannot benefit from additional external funds, and such money may actually weaken the sense of ownership and achievement which is the main result of their frugality.

In the simplest form, the members of most groups do no more than contribute a fixed sum every day, week or month, and one of their number takes the 'pot'; the order may be chosen by lot, or by need, or members may bid for an early place in the queue by agreeing to take less than the total amount.

These merry-go-rounds offer little flexibility, and their members often give up when everyone has had their turn for the pot. Those who are fortunate enough to have their turn before the mid-point are effectively borrowing from those whose turn comes later, and these groups often last no longer than one round. They may have an even shorter life if members are either dishonest or unreliable, but such groups are nevertheless used almost everywhere, particularly by women. They have also been formalised, particularly in the southern states of India, where chit funds may have many thousand members and have become substantial financial institutions in their own right. Here again, they have been serving their customers, rich and poor, for generations.

Cooperative Savings and Credit

The so-called 'new world' of micro-finance is not the first attempt to formalise the virtues of traditional methods of intermediation with a social rather than a business motive. Friedrich Raiffeisen started the first formal cooperative savings and credit organisations in Germany in 1848, and the first Indian Cooperative Credit Societies Act was passed in 1904. These early and genuine Cooperative banking institutions grew up as smaller local groups came together to pool their funds and their expertise, and to facilitate intermediation between savers and borrowers beyond the local community.

Cooperatives and credit unions have in some places continued both to grow and to serve the poor, and in many countries, and districts, they are the most important and successful financial institutions. Elsewhere however, and particularly in the poorer countries, cooperatives have been 'hijacked' by the less poor, the landowners, and by allied political interests. Governments first became involved because of the need to protect needy people from unscrupulous or incompetent promoters, but this very proper concern has often been corrupted by politicians' desire to protect and further their own interests.

Rural cooperatives have also traditionally served farmers, who own some land, however little. There are more and more people who live in rural areas but who own no land at all, and they are increasingly earning their living from activities which have little or even nothing to do with agriculture. These people find it difficult to fit into the usual cooperative financial systems, since their patterns of financial needs and their assets are so different.

The New Wave

Traditional savings and credit mechanisms have thus existed all over the world for hundreds of years, and have been the basis of important financial institutions of many different forms. Why then is there such worldwide interest in micro-finance, and what is different about the new microfinance institutions, some of which are described in this book? Microfinance is in fact a very traditional and familiar form of business, which has evolved and indeed is still evolving in a variety of different ways to meet the needs of its many different customers; what, if anything, is new?

The development business, like most endeavours, is a creature of fashion, and micro-finance is certainly fashionable. There are however a number of good reasons for the fashion, which may mean that the enthusiasm will survive longer than some others appear to have done.

There has been great economic progress in most of the poorer countries of the world, such that many of them can genuinely be called 'developing countries' rather than stagnant or declining ones, The poorer people in most of these countries, however, are relatively and often absolutely worse off than they were ten and even twenty years ago. As populations have increased and the quantity of fertile land has remained the same or has even decreased, more and more people are forced to make a living in some way other than through farming.

Some migrate to the cities in search of employment, but government and public enterprises are 'down-sizing' and in spite of economic liberalisation and restructuring private businesses, whether foreign or local, are not absorbing even a small proportion of the people who want jobs.[1] As a result, the only option is some form of self-employment, whether in the countryside or in the town, and the so-called 'informal sector', or micro-enterprise, appears not to be a temporary waiting place for 'proper' jobs, but a permanent and growing part of the economy.

There have been numerous attempts to provide assistance to small enterprises, but few have been successful. Programmes which are designed to help formal small businesses with services such as training, premises or technical advice are usually neither useful nor economic for informal micro-enterprises, and they can never reach more than a very small proportion of the enterprises they are intended to help.

Micro-finance, however, seems to be the ideal development assistance 'product', It can reach millions of the poorest people, and it can eventually pay for itself, so that the local or foreign development agency can claim to have left behind a permanent self-sustaining institution, which will continue to perform its function without further aid. It goes beyond the traditional test of cost-effectiveness, and can even become a profitable business in its own right.

Micro-finance can also claim another virtue. Its main customers, and indeed those who not only gain the most from it but are best able to make it profitable, are women. Every proposal for a development project has to include a statement as to how it will affect women, but projects for micro-finance cause no problems in this area. It can clearly be demonstrated that women gain economically and that their social position is also improved through access to micro-finance. 'Empowerment' is as difficult to define, and perhaps therefore as popular, as sustainability, but it does seem to be a by-product of successful micro-finance.

Some enthusiasts even argue that micro-finance offers a unique opportunity to combine genuine humanitarian aid for the poorest with good opportunities for trade and investment. Multinational banks are beginning to study its possibilities not as a form of public relations or charity, but as a source of profitable investment opportunities. If 'we' can help the poor by including them in 'our' global financial system, perhaps we never need feel guilty and they will never threaten us again. It is not surprising, therefore, that such an attractive field was in early 1997 accorded the ultimate accolade of a 'summit'.

CHAPTER 2

INTEREST RATES

All the case studies are about micro-finance operations that are at least in some sense profitable, even though subsidies in some cases conceal the real profit potential. Traditional moneylenders, however, who are the original micro-financiers, have always been profitable, so profitability in itself is nothing new. What is new, some critics argue, is that respectable and indeed widely admired micro-finance institutions are charging interest rates which until recently would have been considered usurious.

In many cases, in fact, their rates are in excess of the maximum allowed by laws which control usury, and the institutions have to conceal their true interest rates. Some, particularly in Islamic societies, make borrowers pay some part of the interest as 'administrative charges'. Others charge interest as if the whole loan was outstanding for the whole term, when it is actually being repaid in regular instalments so that the maximum amount is only outstanding for the first period. This method of quoting rates on a flat basis but charging them on the declining balance can be said to be deceptive, but, some would suggest, the deception is forgiven in the general enthusiasm for any form of sustainable development institution. The poor have always paid more for credit as well as for other goods and services; we must be sure that formal micro-finance is not merely a legitimate form of a traditional injustice.

In most of the case studies, the only alternative source of finance which is available to the clients of the institution which is described is the local moneylender. He (or she) may lend money, or he may provide materials or other inputs and then buy back the processed items, in such a way that the person without capital pays a premium over the price of the material for access to credit. The interest rates are sometimes well over 100 per cent per year, but in other cases they are more reasonable, and may be little higher than the rates charged by the formal micro-finance institution.

There are of course other ways in which moneylenders may be less attractive than a formal institution with a development agenda. They may demand that prospective borrowers, and particularly women, should re-affirm their inferior social status as suppliants before their applications are accepted, or they may impose intolerable burdens on defaulters, leading in some cases to perpetual indebtedness and associated bonded labour. We should not necessarily assume, however, that 'new' micro-finance is necessarily a better deal than the alternatives.

What is the 'Market' Rate ?

What is usually clear is that the option of borrowing from a commercial bank or other formal institution was generally not an option at all for the majority of clients of micro-finance institutions. When we speak of 'market rates' of interest we must remember that for most of these clients their 'market' was never the one with which 'we' are familiar. Their market is the moneylender, the local trader or commission agent, or family and friends, and their 'market rate' was whatever rate of interest the accessible sources charged.

This market rate may be in the hundreds or even thousands of per cent per year, or it may be close to the rate charged by a micro-finance institution; whatever it is, we must compare the new rates with that, and not with the bank rates which were never accessible to such borrowers. One of the golden rules of micro-finance is that access is more important to small borrowers than cost, and most of the institutions described in these case studies have provided far better access than typical commercial or development banks. They have done this through ingenious design and good management, but also by charging higher interest rates.

The Effects of Subsidised 'Schemes'

There are, or have been, in most countries, special schemes through which poor people, particularly in rural areas, can take loans. These loans are usually at very low rates of interest, and are thus loss makers for the banks, but they have also failed to achieve their development objectives. Many studies have shown that the total cost to the borrower of a loan from such a scheme is usually well over the cost from a moneylender, because of the delays, the cost of travel, the bribes and other associated problems.

Loans under these schemes are also often tied to particular activities or inputs, which have not been chosen by the borrowers and may not be suitable for them. This only exacerbates the problem of non-repayment, which is itself often abetted by political interests, and the result is that few people benefit, whatever credit culture that may have existed is destroyed and the banks are forced into massive losses. Bankers come to regard banking for the poor as political chicanery, as charity, or as a necessary but loss-making government-mandated necessity. A more damaging combination could scarcely be imagined.

The result is that the field is more or less empty. Liberalisation and structural adjustment are forcing governments to reduce funding for subsidised credit and bankers have been discouraged by years of losses.

There is at the same time a growing need for financial services, as the household economies of even the poorest families become monetised and more and more people need investment capital to enable them to make better use of their shrinking land or to try to make a living from a non-farm business. There is thus a growing need for micro-finance, and the official supply, inadequate as it has always been, is reducing. This vacuum may mean that almost any apparently innovative and potentially sustainable micro-finance system will be welcomed.

This danger is particularly acute in the matter of interest rates. In most places moneylenders' interest rates are far higher than is needed to sustain any reasonably managed formal operation. Although the total financial and non-financial transaction cost for the borrower of a moneylender loan, or a loan from a new micro-finance institution, may be lower than for a loan from a traditional bank, the cost may still be far higher than it need be. We must be discriminating, and be sure that the new micro-finance systems are efficient, that they deliver good value for money, and that the vacuum does not admit new forms of exploitation.

What Can the Customers Afford ?

Poor people have paid high rates of interest since time immemorial. They would not have been able to do this, nor would money lending have survived as a business, if the cost of money had been totally unaffordable. We must therefore examine the issue of ability to pay; how much can small borrowers afford to pay for credit ?

One way of looking at this issue is to examine the way in which poor people use finance, whether it is their own or borrowed. Micro-credit is often perceived mainly as finance for micro-enterprise, although many of the smallest loans in particular are used for so-called 'consumption' purposes. The distinction between 'production' and 'consumption' is in many ways a false one. Expenditure on food or medicine allows people to work, and thus to earn money. Clothing can also be viewed as a productive investment, in that someone who is decently clad is more able to go out for work than someone whose only garment may be so torn, or so dirty, that she has to stay at home.

Poor people also borrow to finance their children's education, whether for fees, or for uniforms, books or other incidentals without which attendance is impossible. This may not have a rapid return, but education, particularly at the primary level, is probably the most productive long-term investment that any society, and thus any member of it, can make.

It is of course difficult to assess the return on investments such as these, and thus to assess what borrowers can afford to pay to finance them. When poor people start to access micro-finance, whether from their own informal ROSCAs or formal institutions, their first loans are usually for 'consumption' purposes of this sort. This is also the first, and perhaps the most important, use for moneylenders' loans as well. We may therefore be able to do no more than assume that people's ability to pay high rates of interest for such purposes means that they can pay.

The Returns from Micro-enterprise

Micro-enterprises, however, are businesses, in which people invest capital in the hope of return. The price that people can afford to pay for this form of investment capital is therefore a function of what they can earn from it. Such businesses generally have no written accounts from which it would be possible to calculate the investment, the profit and therefore the return.

It is however possible to obtain rough but usable data from enterprises of this sort through personal contact. An hour or two of focused discussion with the owner, combined with perceptive observation of his or her business, can elicit information on the market value of whatever simple fixed assets may be involved, and of the working capital in the form of material stocks, money owed by customers for goods bought on credit, or cash. The figures may not be accurate to the last cent, but they may be more truthful than many audited accounts.

Few owners of micro-enterprises make any distinction between profit and their own wages, but it is similarly possible to obtain information about income and expenditure, and thus to make an estimate of the net earnings. From the point of view of return on investment, the important figure is not what the owner chooses to pay her or himself. What matters is the difference between what the business is earning for its owner, whether it is reinvested or withdrawn, and what he or she could have earned by being employed, as opposed to being self-employed. This is the 'opportunity cost' of the owners' labour, and must be subtracted from the net earnings of the business in order to assess what the owner is gaining as a result of the investment.

The percentage return on investment can then be calculated by relating this difference, if it is a positive one, to the total investment in the enterprise. Effectively, the benefit to the owner from the investment is this additional income.

Data from the Field

Over the last five years, data of this kind have been collected from 215 micro-enterprises, as part of student field work assignments in courses in India and Kenya. The businesses were of all types, and they were selected at random by the students along roadsides, in villages and in urban markets. About one-third were owned by women; this rather high figure was because some of the courses are focused on women's self-employment.

The sample cannot of course claim to be representative of all micro-enterprises, but the figures are at least indicative of what can be expected. The figures for investment was not just whatever sum the owner had put in at the start of the business, but was an estimate of the total investment at the time of the visit, from whatever sources. All the figures were adjusted for seasonality, and the opportunity cost of labour was generously estimated; there were only 37 cases where this was nil, because there were clearly no possible opportunities for the owners to earn any money from employment. In every other case, there was some way in which the owner could have earned something during the time he or she spent on the business. For rural people this was usually casual farm labour, possibly some distance from home, and for city dwellers it was portering, domestic service, garbage picking or other casual work.

Failed businesses were not of course included, because they were not there to be studied, and the figures make no allowance for the risk of failure and loss of the investment and the earning capacity it had generated. Many of the businesses had in fact been in existence for five years or more, and although many of the owners spoke of earlier failures, these did not seem to have involved total loss of the investment. Equipment had been sold, and the working capital had been extracted for reinvestment in another venture.

The average annual incremental return on investment, after subtracting the opportunity cost of labour, was 847 per cent. The returns ranged from minus 480 per cent to plus 19,200 per cent, and only in 40 cases, mainly the larger businesses with investments of over $ 500, was the annual return less than 100 per cent. The return was over 1,000 per cent in 44 cases. There were only ten businesses where the owner would have made more money by being employed.

These figures are startling; large businesses are judged to be remarkably successful if they achieve annual returns on capital invested of over 30 per cent or 40 per cent, and investors in the stock market consider themselves fortunate if they make as much as 25 per cent on their portfolios, even including capital gains. At the most conservative level, the opportunity cost of the capital which our micro-entrepreneurs had chosen to invest in their businesses would presumably be whatever they could earn from putting the money in a savings account in a bank. Here even rates of over ten per cent per year are unusual.

These figures do not mean that the owners of micro-enterprises are rich. Because their investments are very small, even these apparently astronomic returns only amount in most cases to very low earnings, often well below the official poverty line or minimum wage in their respective countries. The figures do mean, however, that people who wish to invest in starting or expanding such businesses can afford to pay apparently high rates for the small sums of capital they need. As with so many commodities, and for similar reasons, the poor have to pay more than

The Impact on the Borrowers

Some simple examples may serve to confirm the apparent paradox, that poor people can afford to pay more than the rich for a resource. Five thousand shillings, or about one hundred dollars, is the total capital employed in a women's hairdressing business in a low income district of Nairobi. The owner earns Sh 10,000 a month from her business, which is Shs 7,000 more than she could earn if she worked in someone else's saloon. She actually borrowed the capital from her family, but if this source had not been available, she would presumably have looked elsewhere.

If she had been able to borrow from a bank she would have at the time had to pay about 18 per cent interest, or Shs 75 a month, for the necessary capital. If she had borrowed from one of the new micro-finance institutions, however, she would probably have had to pay about 38 per cent interest, or about Sh 160 a month. This is Shs 85 more than the cost from a bank, but it is less than one per cent of her monthly earnings. This woman, however, did not have the option of borrowing from a bank. The choice for her would not have been between a bank and the new institution, but between the new institution or not at all. Clearly, the investment is still highly profitable in spite of the apparently high interest rate.

Another woman makes bamboo sleeping mats in a village in Tamil Nadu in South India. She has invested ten thousand rupees, or about $ 280, in her business, and earns about two thousand rupees a month from it; without the business, she could only earn about three hundred rupees from casual labour. The bank has a scheme through which such people can take loans for business, and the annual interest rate is about 12 per cent. Very few really needy people ever get these loans, however, and the women has borrowed her capital from a self-help group to which she belongs. She is paying three per cent interest a month, which amounts to 300 rupees. This is a substantial sum, but it is still only 15 per cent of her monthly income, and she is clearly better off than she would have been without the business.

A few of the 215 businesses for which this information was obtained were much larger than these two examples, although most were smaller. As might have been expected, the return on the investment in the larger businesses was generally much lower than for the smaller ones, and their owners could not have afforded higher interest rates such as the figures of 30 per cent and 38 per cent in the above examples. This merely reinforces the point that micro-finance is for micro-businesses, which are usually owned by people with micro-incomes. The interest rates that the new institutions have to charge to cover their costs in themselves discourage better-off people from 'hijacking' their services .

The case studies include many other such examples. They do not justify inefficiency, and it is obviously better for a poor person to pay less for her capital, if it is possible. The figures suggest, however, that borrowers who invest in micro-enterprises, and particularly the smallest ones, can afford to pay the high rates of interest which are being charged. No financial system can survive unless every link in the chain is profitable, and our data, like the numerous examples in the case studies, show that the final link, the person whom the whole system is intended to assist, can be profitable. The case studies in this book provide an opportunity to judge which forms of intermediation which deliver the service can be similarly sustainable.

CHAPTER 3

WHERE IS THE MONEY TO COME FROM ?

There is therefore an 'effective demand' for credit; poor people need to borrow, and the returns on their small investments are high enough to enable them to pay the prices which lenders need to charge. Financial intermediation, however, is not just about lending; the sources of funds must be as sustainable as their use.

The origins of financial intermediation are within local communities; some people need to save and others need to borrow, and their differing requirements are satisfied first through individual transactions and then, quite soon, through some form of intermediation. It might appear that this form of circulation of money would be inappropriate for poor communities, where nobody, by definition, has more money than he or she needs.

The Need to Save

In fact, however, the need to save is not so much a function of surplus funds as of insecurity. In a household where even one day's sickness can lead to immediate hunger, or where daily earnings depend on the weather or the whims of a local landowner, it is vital to have some means of saving. The need to save is matched by the inability to invest. Poor people can spend, but one of the main reasons for their poverty is their lack of opportunities to invest profitably. Their lack of resources, skills and information mean that they cannot use loans which they know they will have to repay; their need to save is matched by their inability to borrow.

Many poor people have savings accounts with commercial banks, but this form of saving has numerous disadvantages, particularly for women. Bank branches may be inconveniently located and their opening hours are fixed for the convenience of their staff rather than for people who must work throughout the day. Many banks refuse to open savings accounts below a certain minimum amount, which may be very substantial for a small saver, and they may also require that a certain minimum balance is maintained. They may not pay any interest on small accounts, or may even force their depositors to close their accounts if they fall below this level.

Even small depositors may be required to provide references, and to go through formalities which bewilder people who are unused to formal procedures, particularly if they are illiterate, which most poor women in many countries are. Some small rural banks are modest and their staff deal courteously and sensitively with new customers who have never had any previous contact with a formal institution. In other cases. however, the very premises are intimidating; armed guards stand at the door, and once a newcomer has dared to pass them the staff treat him with contempt and disdain. Urgent withdrawals may also be difficult, and depositors may be required to produce some written proof of identity, such as a ration card, which they cannot obtain.

Post offices offer an alternative in some countries, but they resemble the banks in many ways, and their security is not always beyond question. In some countries governments have allowed post office savings banks to fail. One advantage of saving with a bank is that the saver may eventually become eligible for credit. Post office savings banks, as their name implies, only offer savings.

ROSCAs and other traditional informal financial systems have to offer some members a savings facility if others are to be able to borrow. The two services are complementary, and the term 'micro-credit', which was the label for the 'summit' in early 1997, is a misnomer, unless it is taken to refer to the credit given to the institution by savers as well as the credit taken by borrowers.

Nevertheless, few of the newer micro-finance institutions rely to any substantial extent on their own clients' savings as a source of funds. Most of the new institutions were initially funded by donors, and many still rely on this source for new money. The banking laws of most countries quite rightly demand that only very sound and well-established institutions are allowed to take deposits, particularly from small savers. A few non-government organisations, including some described in this book, have evaded these laws in various ways, but only in a few cases do client savings, however described, provide more than a small proportion of the funds which are lent.

In the long term, however, the new wave of micro-finance institutions can be expected to move closer to the traditional models from which they claim they have evolved, and client savings will make up the major share of their financial resources. This will reduce their dependence on outside sources of finance, whether they are subsidised or not, and will also enhance their clients' sense of identification with the institution.

Funds from the Existing Banking System

Commercial banks have traditionally mobilised low-cost deposits from poorer people, and particularly from rural areas, and have lent the money to urban dwellers who are better off and have more access to investment opportunities. The briefest inspection of the balance sheet of any bank in a poor rural area will show that this situation is unchanged, and it may be premature to expect funds to flow from the centre to the periphery when the present flow is so strongly in the reverse direction. Perhaps the first priority should be to reduce the scale of the present flow.

As the case studies show, however, some banks are starting to 'push' funds towards poorer customers, as well as encouraging them to save. They may be lending small amounts to individual borrowers, or in some cases they are treating groups of small borrowers as a new form of customer. This reduces the bankers' transaction costs by aggregating the borrowings, as well as the repayments and the savings, of several small clients into one account. The groups can also be used in a variety of ways to provide the security that is quite beyond the capacity of the individual member. Some development and commercial banks are also starting to wholesale funds through non-government organisations or federations of client groups, thus further reducing their costs.

In nearly every case, however, banks are lending to poorer people, whether directly or indirectly, not because they have decided that small clients are a valuable new customer group from which they can generate profitable business. They are doing it because governments demand that they should, because it is good 'public relations', or because they have received cheap funds or other subsidies which are tied to this form of lending and which make it profitable.

Readers must decide for themselves whether this is the only way in which banks can ever serve this enormous market, or whether there is money to be made by doing business with the poor, in a way which serves the interest of all parties.

Donor Funds, Grants and Subsidies

The last category of funding, which for most of the institutions described in the case studies was the first, is not commercial. It includes support from government sources and charitable organisations, whether domestic or foreign, and may come in the form of grants, subsidised loans, gifts in kind such as training, vehicles or computers, or 'patient equity', where investors are prepared to accept a low and long delayed return on their money because of the social goals they expect the institution to achieve.

The very fact that this kind of support has been necessary to 'kick-start' the new wave of micro-finance initiatives, and that it may continue to be necessary in many cases if the institutions are to survive, suggests that micro-finance is not fundamentally profitable. If it was so profitable, it can be argued, traditional money-lending would have evolved into an important and responsible sector of the finance industry.

In a sense, of course, it has. Southern Indian chit funds constitute a large and highly profitable business which has evolved from traditional merry-go-rounds and ROSCAs, and in Western Europe and North America credit cards, hire purchase and other forms of lending have developed to provide credit to people who for some reason either cannot or do not want to borrow from a bank. Their interest rates are often twice as high as bank overdrafts or term loans, but because of their convenience and their lenient security requirements they have taken a major share of the credit marketplace.

These systems, however, have generally not reached poorer people and they have usually not reached more than a very small percentage of the population in the poorer countries. Governments' well-intentioned attempts to protect vulnerable people from exploitation have often discouraged the development of appropriate financial services. As we have seen, small borrowers can afford to pay higher than 'normal' rates of interest, and lenders need to charge high rates to serve them properly.

In many countries so-called usury laws forbid lenders to charge interest above a certain minimum, and this is usually set at a rate which is insufficient to cover the cost of service to small borrowers. Loans at above this rate are illegal and defaulters cannot be taken to law. The result is that poorer borrowers are served by illegal lenders; these lenders cannot expand because they must remain invisible, and they cannot legally access deposits. They are thus denied the benefits of economies of scale, and they must add a premium to their interest rates to cover the risk of prosecution and the cost of being denied access to legal methods of recovery. Even in the United Kingdom, so-called 'loan sharks' exist in all the major cities; they are often linked to the underworld of drug dealing and crime, and some authorities devote more effort to stopping them than to promoting more equitable and legal alternatives.

For many reasons, therefore, there appears to be a need for subsidy. The current enthusiasm for micro-finance may indeed mean that some institutions will be deprived of the opportunity to demonstrate their sustainability because the continuing flow of subsidy makes it unnecessary.

Subsidy can take many forms, some of which are more damaging than others. Many of the 'new generation' of micro-finance institutions owe their origins to donor-funded 'projects' where there was no question of any repayment or financial return on the investment; the process of project appraisal would, or should, have satisfied the donor that the social or economic benefits would exceed the costs. There may not even have been any concern for sustainability; if a project achieves its planned results within the given time frame and budget, there is no reason why it should necessarily be converted into a permanent institution.

When the explicit objective from the start is to create a sustainable financial institution, however, the funds which are provided to cover its initial costs, and to be lent, are analogous to venture capital for a profit seeking business. There is no guarantee that the enterprise will succeed, but if it does, the investor expects large returns. The difference is that a private investor expects dividends and capital gains, whereas the donor presumably expects large and continuing benefits to whatever 'target group' is intended to benefit.

As micro-finance institutions move towards sustainability, they are expected to cover an increasing proportion of their costs from earnings, mainly in the form of interest paid by borrowers. Subsidies continue, however, in a variety of forms. Loan funds may be given in the form of grants, which are not repayable and will eventually form the equity base of the new institution; dividends will not however have to be paid on them. Alternatively, the institutions may be given interest-free or heavily subsidised loan funds, so that they can make a larger 'spread', or gross profit margin, on their loans, while they are moving towards genuine sustainability.

Finally, and often many years after they have claimed sustainability, micro-finance institutions still receive subsidy in kind. This may come in the form of free training or travel, gifts of equipment or simple untied donations, from agencies or individuals. It is in fact very hard for any institution which has remained true to its original social mission to become totally sustainable.

Donors have to continue to donate to justify their existence, and an institution which is covering all its costs is not therefore necessarily any less deserving of charity.

The case study institutions in this book are all receiving subsidy of some kind, although in most cases they are less dependent on it than when they started. Readers must decide for themselves which sorts of subsidy are least damaging, or most helpful.

Forced savings should be minimised, and the real cost of loans should not be inflated, whether by mis-statements of interest rates or by excessive or over-complex savings requirements.

CHAPTER 4

THE INSTITUTIONS

The Importance of Institutional 'Fit'

In micro-finance, as in so many fields, the institution that does the job may be more important than the details of the job itself. There are certainly many examples of well-designed programmes which have failed because the implementing institutions were unable to manage them properly, as well as successes which clearly owed more to the competence of the institution than to the virtues of the programme itself. Mismanagement may be the fault of incompetent managers rather than of the institution as a whole, but the wrong institution, even with the best managers, is unlikely to be able to make a success of a micro-finance programme, however well it has been designed.

Sustainability is usually understood in a financial sense; if a programme is able to cover its costs, it is said to be sustainable. Over the long term, however, this is no more than one indicator of institutional sustainability, or continuing long-term ability to manage the programme so that it both maintains its mission and is financially sustainable. Many of the best known micro-finance programmes have been initiated and are still run by 'social entrepreneurs' or 'charismatic leaders'. They are individuals of unusual vision and ability who can inspire others to work with them and support them. It may be every bit as difficult to eliminate dependence on such a person and to create a managerially sustainable institution as it was to start the programme at the beginning, or to bring it to what may be only short-term financial sustainability.

The Institutional Alternatives

The ideal institution to deliver financial services to smaller users is one which can initiate and develop the activity and then carry it on for as long as it is needed. This is almost certain to be longer than the working lifetime of whoever started it.

Institutions evolve and change their legal form. The case studies include examples of micro-finance institutions at every stage of their development. Some are just starting, while others are well-established with a track record of success. Their institutional forms reflect these differences. Some are no more than informal groups, while others are full-fledged banks. Growth and the need for continuity make different demands, and it may be appropriate at a certain stage to convert an NGO into a bank or other form of financial institution. Alternatively, what started as one component of a large range of different welfare services may develop to the level where it should be 'spun off' and constituted into a separate organisation, of whatever kind is appropriate.

Flexibility is necessary in the early stages of any innovation, but as micro-finance matures into an industry it should be less necessary for new institutions to have to go through the stresses of transformation. Their culture and informal systems will change, but the initial legal and organisational form may be able to remain in place.

Although micro-finance is now an industry, it is a very small and fragile one, and its services have only reached a tiny proportion of the people who can benefit from them. The total number of borrowers from the institutions which are members of the recently established Microfinance Network was under four million at the end of 1995, and if the two Indonesian and Bangladeshi members are excluded, the total is reduced to 213,000. Only three of the sixteen institutions which are described in these case studies are members of this Network, but these figures do show how far there is to go, and how great is the need for new entrants to the market.

Government

Until the late 1970s, development was considered to be governments' responsibility, and if new services were necessary, government would set up its own departments and offices to provide them. Colonial regimes, and their banks, had often failed to deliver credit to indigenous people, and numerous heavily subsidised schemes were started to fill the gaps. In some cases the banks were used to disburse loans and collect such repayments as were made, but in others the government undertook the whole operation.

The results were usually disastrous, and it is now generally agreed that banking is the business of banks. The issue in micro-finance is not whether government should become more directly involved, but whether expansion will come from the banks, from existing NGOs or from totally new institutions.

The Commercial Banks

The existing commercial banks are the first choice to undertake a rapid expansion of micro-finance. Most obviously, they are already there. Coverage varies between countries, but there are hundreds of thousands of retail banks in the developing countries. Every city and major town is covered, and there are also outlets in most rural areas. They have the necessary security equipment for handling cash, and the branches are served by a hierarchy of administrative systems which ensure that correct records are kept and that a minimum level of service is provided.

People are more important than physical infrastructure. The banks have staff who know how to administer and manage savings and lending operations. They may need training in new techniques of micro-finance, but they have the necessary basic skills. Bankers are often criticised for their conservatism and lack of imagination, but they are known for their concern for detail and for correct calculations, and some sort of administrative discipline is maintained even in the weakest banks.

Micro-finance has thus far been mainly concerned with innovation, and funding for most institutions has come from donors or development funds. In the future, most funds will have to come from deposits from the same people who are also the borrowers, and this will require rather different attitudes. Creativity and initiative are not necessarily the ideal qualities for people whose job is to take care of other people's money. Governments are rightly reluctant to allow young and untried institutions to solicit deposits, particularly small savings, but the banks already perform this function rather well. Profitable lending is the obvious complement to the existing savings relationship.

Most low income people have never used banks' services of any kind, and most of those who are bank customers use them for saving rather than borrowing. Nearly everyone, however, is aware that banks exist and that they do lend money. The banks have not had difficulty in generating demand for credit from the large number of misconceived and thus unsuccessful loan 'schemes' which have been imposed on them by the state in so many countries. It should therefore be possible for the same banks to market the new forms of micro-financial services.

National commercial banks also need new markets. Until recently they have been able to cross-subsidise their rural business with profits from large corporate clients and government. Rural branches could be treated as centres for deposit mobilisation, and the funds could be lent profitably through their urban networks. As financial markets are liberalised, however, the international banks are entering previously protected markets; local banks may find that their extensive rural branch networks offer their best or perhaps even their only opportunity for expansion, and they can use the new approaches to micro-finance to make this business profitable.

There are thus many good reasons why the existing commercial banks should take over the task of 'scaling up' micro-finance, building on the results that have been achieved by institutions such as those described in these case studies. As in many fields, radical changes have to be introduced by new organisations, but once the technologies have been proved, the older and larger organisations can take over.

Only one case study in this book, however, is about a programme which is being operated by a large commercial bank. Apart from the village unit of the National Bank of Indonesia, the other cases describe the micro-finance operations of new institutions, or of specialised development banks such as the Regional Rural banks in India, most of which are small. The new era of micro-finance started over twenty years ago, if we take 1976, the year in which the operations of what later became Grameen Bank started in Bangladesh in 1976, as its beginning. Banks are conservative institutions, but one might have thought that more than one major programme might have started in that period. If we judge institutional suitability by what has actually happened, the commercial banks are not the first choice.

This demonstrates that people's attitudes and beliefs are more important than their skills and the physical infrastructure they have to work with. The social distance between most bankers and the poor is enormous, and bankers have been conditioned to believe that the only way to ensure that people will repay loans is to take security of the equivalent or higher value. Their experience with government and donor-sponsored programmes has reinforced the point; the poor are not bankable.

The poor themselves have come to share the same view. Most micro-enterprise owners never even consider going to a bank for finance. They themselves, or people known to them, may have taken loans through government sponsored schemes where repayment is the exception rather than the rule, particularly for people with the right connections. The administrative hurdles, the delays and incidental costs are also often such as to discourage small borrowers. Numerous studies have shown that it is actually cheaper for such people to borrow at very high rates of interest from moneylenders, because the final cost of a bank loan is even higher.

The ownership of commercial banks is also not such as to encourage marginalised people to think they can borrow money from them on a business-like basis. The banks may be controlled by government, which is often regarded as an erratic but occasionally generous source of handouts rather than as a partner in business transactions. Alternatively, they are owned by local or international investors whose natural focus is perceived to be the wealthy modern sector rather than on the poor.

In sum, therefore, the perceptions of bank staff and of their prospective micro-finance customers are not such as to encourage them to do business with each other.

Non-Government Organisations

NGOs have so far been the main innovators in micro-finance. Will they continue to dominate the new industry which they have created, or will the banks overcome their weaknesses and move into this new field for which they are in so many ways ideally equipped ?

Some NGOs have succeeded in scaling up their activities and reaching large numbers. One of the largest micro-finance programmes, anywhere, is run by the Bangladesh Rural Advancement Committee (BRAC), which is an NGO. The BRAC micro-finance operation reaches over one-and-a-half million people. It is now proposed to separate it from the rest of the organisation and incorporate it as a fully-fledged bank, but its NGO status has not so far seriously inhibited its growth. KREP in Kenya is one of the bigger micro-finance institutions in Africa with over 15,000 clients. Here again, it is proposed to convert it into a bank, but its present success has been achieved as an NGO.

NGOs have many other advantages. Their very name, 'non-government', demonstrates their flexibility. They are defined only by what they are not, which suggests that they can be whatever they need to be for a particular purpose. This is of course not entirely true, in that private profit-seeking businesses are not normally considered as NGOs although the name does not exclude this possibility. Nevertheless, NGOs can and do undertake all manner of different trading activities which might be thought to demand different organisational forms; micro-finance, or money-lending, is one of them.

Donors, and national governments, now regard NGOs as the most appropriate institutions through which to deliver development services. Many NGOs which used to pursue their own agenda, funded by private donations, have now become sub-contractors to governments; the majority of donor-funded micro-finance projects are in fact implemented by NGOs, rather than by banks. Some banks are themselves funding NGO micro-finance projects with grants and cheap loans. They may be criticised for treating a profitable business opportunity as a public relations gesture, but they do recognise the flexibility and strength of the organisations they fund. Whatever the source, NGOs are in a position to access funds which would not be available to governments, or to banks.

Professional managers are also beginning to regard NGOs as appropriate employers. Their salary levels are still below the highest in the private sector, but they are no longer at the level of semi-volunteers; it may be significant that the term 'NGO' has largely replaced 'PVO' or Private Voluntary Organisation, since their staff no longer work for nothing and their funding is no longer mainly voluntary.

The best NGOs differ in one very significant way from businesses. They aim not to secure their own future and growth, but to enable their clients to take control over their own destinies. This often means that the NGO has to withdraw from its most successful activities, because their success is in part measured by their client communities' ability to manage without further assistance.

Some of the micro-finance institutions in these case studies have almost reached this condition; it may not be appropriate for every community to own and manage its own bank, any more than it should have its own rice mill or bus. If it is the right thing, however, an NGO is far more likely to make it happen than a commercial bank or a government department.

An NGO is also likely to be able to decide whether this is the right thing to do. The case studies here show how many different ways there are of delivering financial services to poor communities. Commercial firms, including banks, undertake market research to discover the needs of their prospective customers and to test new products. NGOs try to address people's needs in a more holistic way, through participative techniques and through living with and being a part of the communities which they serve. It is easy to exaggerate the extent to which NGOs 'know' their communities, and most NGO staff are from a very different social background to that of the people with whom they work. Nevertheless, poor people's needs for financial services are more complex and more interwoven with their whole livelihood than their needs for soap or soft drinks. A competent NGO can identify and address them more effectively than a bank.

NGOs have their own disadvantages, however, which are becoming more evident as they move into unfamiliar roles. They have access to donations, but this strength can also be a weakness. The donors themselves may object to their funds being used for loans to poor people rather than gifts, particularly at what appear to be high rates of interest with an uncharitable insistence on repayment. Some staff may share these views, and will resist head office pressure to change their view. Clients who are used to receiving grants, even if they are matched by local contributions, will find it difficult to understand when the same agency starts to act like a moneylender.

Many NGO staff are reluctant to accept that profit-seeking businesses can contribute to social goals, except perhaps through contributions to 'good causes' such as their own NGOs. Micro-finance can only be successful if borrowers invest their loans in profitable enterprises, and individually-owned businesses, even at the smallest scale, are more likely to be successful than group or cooperative enterprises. Some NGOs equate employment with exploitation, and will only promote community enterprises where the workers are also the owners. There are some isolated instances where this type of business has dramatically succeeded, but they are few and far between. It is impossible to build a sound financial institution if the portfolio excludes the type of businesses that most people prefer to undertake, and which are most likely to succeed.

Successful micro-finance requires managers who welcome the owners of profitable business as clients but who also strive to make profits for their own institution. The distinction between sustainability and profitability is a fine one. A sound financial institution must have equity as well as debt. A genuinely sustainable institution must be able to cover its operating costs, to pay interest on the money it borrows to on-lend, and to earn a return on the equity, in order to finance its own growth and to compensate for the effect of inflation.

Donor funds and fashion have been driving NGOs into micro-finance. Some whose staff are uncertain about the social benefits of profits have been wise enough to remain in the field of welfare where their services are still so desperately needed, but some have been unable to resist the temptation, and their failure has not only damaged themselves but it has also made it more difficult for programmes with 'hard-headed' management to succeed. In 'real' business, a firm whose prices are too low to cover its costs, or which allows its customers not to pay their bills, rapidly disappears. Micro-finance, however, is not yet a 'real' business, and there are many NGO- and government-sponsored micro-finance programmes which are allowed to survive in spite of bad management. The weak credit culture which they create makes it harder for well-managed institutions to survive.

NGOs are usually started by visionaries who are motivated by an ideal which transcends personal wealth. They may attract like-minded colleagues, but the expansion and development of a successful financial business needs more than a charismatic leader. Some pioneers recognise this and leave, while others may be seduced away by the lure of international acclaim. The conferences which they adorn often achieve little in themselves, but one result may be that their leader's absence forces second-line management to take over responsibility. Very often, however, social entrepreneurs make the same mistake as business ones; they cannot 'let go', and their organisations can never evolve into managerially self-sustaining institutions.

No one type of institution is the right one for scaling-up micro-finance. Institutions differ more because of who runs and staffs them than because of their legal form, and both banks and NGOs have succeeded in starting and massively expanding micro-financial services. The ideal may be a completely new institution, such as those described in some of the case studies, which is formed specifically for the purpose and thus avoids the cultural 'hangovers' that make it so difficult for existing organisations of any kind to move successfully into this new field.

The problem here, of course, is that it takes a long time to establish a new institution, and, like any new enterprise, the proportion which survive and grow is very small indeed. The need is urgent, and bankers in particular should try to overcome their inhibitions in order to enter the field. It is hoped that the case studies which follow will suggest ways in which this can be done.

Section 2

CASE STUDIES

CHAPTER 5

BHAWAL RAJBARI BRANCH, GRAMEEN BANK BANGLADESH

The Bhawal Rajbari branch of Grameen Bank Bangladesh was established in 1982, some six years after the Bank was started. It was the thirty-second branch of the Bank to be set up, and is situated in Gazipur District, about 60 km North of Dhaka. The bank's borrowers are organised into groups of five members; up to seven or eight such groups then form a centre, which meets every week and is the forum through which the Bank meets its customers.

Although their financial transactions are carried out within the groups, the great majority of the actual activities for which the loans from the Bank provide the necessary capital are carried out on an individual basis. They include a vast range of different enterprises, such as petty trading, rice'processing, raising animals, and hundreds of others. Some activities, however, are undertaken on a group basis by some or all of the members of a Group or Centre.

Centre 39 was started in 1983, one year after the Bhawal Rajbari branch was established. All the 35 members are women, and they all live in the same small settlement about 4 km away from Rajbari village and 3 km away from the Grameen Bank branch. The Bank's membership regulations mean that all the women come from landless or virtually landless families. Most of them have small gardens beside their huts, and before they joined Grameen Bank the only way in which they could earn any money to supplement the wretchedly low and irregular wages they could earn by working for other farmers was by keeping a few chickens or goats by their homes.

Since the women have been able to borrow from the Grameen Bank most of them have bought cows. An in-calf cow costs 6,000 taka, which they can now afford by taking a loan for 5,000 taka and making up the balance from their own savings. When the cow gives birth the one-third of its milk which is not used by the calf or the family is sold for about 12 taka a day, which is just enough to cover the weekly loan repayments of 100 taka. At the end of the year, they either sell the cow and the calf, or keep both, or sell one and keep one; either way, their loan is cleared and they have acquired a valuable asset.

By 1991 the women had developed a strong sense of solidarity as a result of their eight years of association with the Bank. Only five new members had joined the Centre, to replace five who had died or left the area. One member died in 1987 still owing 3,000 taka. Her husband repaid the loan by selling one of the family's cows, but the members unanimously agreed to give him a lump sum of the same amount, which they withdrew from the Emergency Fund which they had built up as part of the Grameen Bank's lending and repayment process.

In 1990 all the women agreed to undertake a joint venture, as well as continuing with their own individual cattle raising. They jointly borrowed 35,000 taka which they then paid for a three-month lease on a small jackfruit plantation with twenty fruit-bearing trees. The owner was willing to lease out the field because he needed ready cash and he did not want to have to hire labour and organise the marketing. The members of Centre 39, however, knew that this work would not conflict with their other tasks.

The women had calculated that they would be able to sell the ripe fruit for about 50,000 taka. As it turned out, however, thieves started to steal the unripe fruit almost at once. The women quickly decided to sell the fruit earlier than planned, in order to avoid further losses, even though meant that they would get a lower price. They sold the fruit for 39,000 taka, less than a month after taking the lease.

After they had repaid the loan of 35,000 taka, and 500 taka as interest for one month, the women had 3,500 taka left over. They shared this equally, so that each member received one hundred taka. They had each worked for the equivalent of about three full days on harvesting and marketing the fruit. The current rate for day labour, with no food included, was about forty taka, but this work was not always available and it often involved travelling some distance. The women were thus reasonably satisfied with their venture, and they agreed to consider another joint venture in the following year.

Centre 23 is a men's group. Like Centre 39, it was started in 1983, and it has 35 members as five groups of seven. They started their joint activities in 1988. They jointly borrowed 136,000 taka to lease a plot of irrigated paddy land, and they earned a good return after repaying their loan. In 1989 they borrowed 35,000 taka to construct a deep tube well with which to irrigate their own small patches of land and those of some of their neighbours, who paid for the service, and this too was a success. In 1990 they could not agree on a common activity so they decided to concentrate on their individual activities, most of which were financed by loans from the Grameen Bank.

In 1991 some members thought that they should do a joint activity again. After some discussion, two groups decided not to, and 24 members of the other five groups, that is all of them except one member who preferred not to be involved, borrowed 43,000 taka to lease a three-acre banana plantation. The owner had already planted and cultivated the trees; all the members had to do was to carry out the final stages of cultivation, to protect the trees from thieves and to transport and sell the ripe fruit.

After two months the members harvested 600 sticks of bananas. They sold the bananas in Dhaka for a total of 72,000 taka, and after paying 120 taka per stick for transport the net proceeds were 60,000 taka. They repaid the 43,000 taka loan, plus 1150 taka interest, leaving a balance of 15,850 taka. Three of the members had travelled with the bananas to Dhaka to sell them, and the other 21 members had each spent about the same amount of time on cultivating, guarding and harvesting the crop. They agreed that each of them should receive 500 taka, which was a very good return for only three or four days work. They deposited the balance of 3,850 taka in their group fund with Grameen Bank, to help them finance future joint activities.

Centre 49, which was started in 1984, is made up of six groups of five women each. They live in a cluster of huts about 3 km away from the Grameen Bank branch. Most of the members make puffed rice which they sell in the local market, and some of them have other income-generating activities such as sewing or rearing cattle. These are all financed with loans from the Grameen Bank.

In 1988 they decided to do a joint activity. They leased an irrigated field and planted paddy. They had a good crop, and they did the same each year thereafter; by March 1991 they had a total of 81,000 taka in the three joint funds which they operated as part of their financing arrangements with Grameen Bank.

In 1991 they decided to lease a larger field of two acres. They borrowed 45,000 taka to pay for the lease, or 1,500 taka for each member, and they also withdrew a further 1,000 taka from their joint savings account to pay for fertiliser. The Centre Chief agreed to take charge of the irrigation system, and all the members, along with their husbands and children, worked together to plant, weed and harvest the paddy.

The first harvest yielded 1,500 kg of paddy. Some of the members who had space in their homes agreed to store the paddy free of charge, and they planned to sell it for 30 taka a kg, or 45,000 taka in total. This would be enough to pay off the principal of the loan, and they estimated that they would be able to sell the second crop for about 24,000 taka. After deducting 4,500 taka for interest and repaying the 1,000 taka to their joint fund, this would leave them with 18,500 taka. They did not plan to distribute this, but to re-invest it in their Group fund so that they could undertake another similarly profitable joint venture the next year.

The Bhawal Rajbari branch, of which all these people were customers, is typical of the older branches of the Grameen Bank. In 1991 it had a total staff of 11 people, and was serving 1,684 members in 384 Groups, which were in turn organised into 69 Centres, such as those described above. In addition, some 300 non-members used the branch for deposit and checking account facilities, since they could earn a marginally higher rate of interest, and receive rather better service, than at the branch of one of the nationalised commercial banks in Rajbari village itself, which lies about one kilometre from the Grameen Bank branch.

The Bhawal Rajbari branch lies quite near the main road from Dhaka to Mymensingh, a large town in the north of Bangladesh, and most of the branch staff come from one or other of these two cities, or from other urban areas. The manager and his bank workers all have university education, and they have all been through the very rigorous field training programme which is designed to expose new recruits to the realities of rural Bangladesh, which are unfamiliar to many urban people, and to the rigours of the daily routine of the Bank's work. Many recruits resign during the training; those that remain are paid at the same rates as government employees of the same background, with the addition of a substantial bonus which is based on their branch performance. In 1991 the staff of the Bhawal Rajbari branch received a bonus of almost ten per cent of their annual wages.

The Grameen Bank branch is in a two-storey building which stands in a field by a small road. One of the two female members of staff is married to one of the staff, and she and her husband, together with the other female staff member, lived in a house near to the branch office building. It is uncommon for single women to work away from home in Bangladesh, and although most of the Grameen Bank's clients, in Bhawal Rajbari and elsewhere, were women, nearly all the staff were men. All the other staff live together on the top floor of the bank building. The manager has a small private bedroom, and the other staff share a dormitory and the common washing and eating facilities.

The office is on the ground floor; there is no banking counter, since most of the banking business is done at the weekly Centre meetings near to the members' homes. Customers only visit the office to receive loan disbursements and to make withdrawals, and when they do this they transact their business at their respective bank worker's desks.

The manager and his staff were proud of their branch's high repayment record, and of the profit of over 160,000 taka which it made in 1991. This was calculated after paying interest on clients' deposits, and the costs also included 134,000 taka of notional interest paid to Grameen bank headquarters on the difference between the deposited funds and the amounts advanced. Since the Grameen Bank actually makes use of large sums of money from foreign subsidised sources, this notional payment covers the costs of the regional, zonal and central headquarters.

The cumulative disbursements of the branch from its inception up to the end of October 1991 are summarised as follows (figures in taka):

	Men	Women	Total
Loans for general activities	36,156,000	102,765,000	138,921,000
Housing loans	5,865,000	16,113,000	21,978,000
Total	42,021,000	118,878,000	160,899,000

The procedure by which the groups and centres are formed, and loans are approved, disbursed and recovered, was as follows:

1) (For new areas) A bank worker spends some time in the village, informing people about the Bank and its methods and requirements for membership.

2) Five interested people, all men or all women, decide to form a group. They approach the bank worker and he meets them at one of their homes, to explain to them in more detail what is involved.

3) If the group are still interested, and the worker believes they need and can benefit from the Bank's services, the Group have seven to ten days training, during which they learn to sign their names and to recite as many as they can of the Banks' 16 slogans about banking and better living, to understand the basic rules of the Bank and to agree on a fixed day, time and place for their weekly meetings. They also have to appoint a Chairperson and Secretary.

4) If the training is successful, the worker visits each applicant at her or his home, and ensures that they qualify as clients in that they own no land or at most half an acre, and are not otherwise disqualified by possessing more than 10,000 taka worth of assets other than their homestead.

5) If all qualify, a programme officer from the Regional office meets the new group with the field worker and gives his approval.

6) The new group is either then added to an existing Centre, which can have from two to eight groups, or forms a new Centre with another new group or one which might leave an existing Centre for this purpose, usually to have a meeting place nearer to members' homes. The Centre agrees on their weekly meeting day, time and place.

7) At the first weekly meeting, each member contributes seven taka to start their 'Special Fund'; that is, they save one taka per day, so a five-member group saves 35 taka a week. They hand over the money to the bank worker, who deposits the money in the branch in order to open their fund.

8) At the second meeting, the same day and time a week later, the members bring their seven taka again, and so on for as long as they are members of their groups and clients of the Bank.

9) After three or four meetings, the groups may submit one or possibly two loan proposals. The maximum is 3,000 taka for the first

loan. The worker may assist the members to prepare their proposals. Additional loan proposals are submitted at later meetings, and the Chairperson and Secretary are expected to be the last to submit their applications.

10) If the worker approves the applications, he hands them over to the branch manager. If the branch manager approves them, they are accumulated with proposals from other groups until each Wednesday evening. The manager takes them to the weekly regional meeting on each Thursday.

11) At the regional meeting the loan proposals are either approved, or, rarely, turned down, and are returned from the regional office by the following Saturday, two days after the meeting, at the latest.

12) The approved loans are disbursed at the branch office to the individual member, or an agreed nominee for group loans, on any day which is convenient to them the following week.

13) The loans must be invested in the proposed activity within the next seven days, unless the borrower's fellow-members agree that this is impractical. Most Centre meetings take place between 7 a.m. and 8 a.m., and last about 30 minutes. Each worker is responsible for up to ten Centres. With a maximum of two meetings every morning he can spend the rest of the morning in the field meeting members and checking on loan utilisation, before returning to the office for lunch, for record-keeping and to make disbursements.

14) Repayments start the week after disbursement, and loans are repaid in fifty equal instalments, plus interest at 16 per cent calculated on the declining balance, regardless of their purpose except for housing loans. Prepayments are permitted. No loan applications can be accepted if any member of a Group is in arrears. Repayments are collected at every weekly meeting together with the seven taka savings contribution.

Clients have to contribute to the following funds as a part of the process of participation in the group-based financial system:

The Group Fund

This fund is made up as follows:

- One taka per week per member, taken from the seven taka per week contribution.
- Five per cent of all loans disbursed, which is deducted from loans at the time of disbursement
- Five per cent of loans disbursed from the group fund itself, again deducted at the time of disbursement.
- Any penalty charges that group members may choose to levy on themselves for late repayment, non-attendance and so on.
- Interest paid by the bank on the fund at 8.5 per cent per year.

Members can borrow up to half this fund for any purpose, such as festivals or entertainment, and they can borrow the balance for joint or individual income-generating activities. No interest is charged, apart from the 5 per cent initial deduction.

The Special Fund

This fund is made up from one taka per week per member, taken from the seven taka per week contribution, and can only be used for purposes which serve the interest of a whole Centre, such as the construction of a meeting place or other community facility. By 1991 the clients of the Bhawal Rajbari branch had built 53 such structures. Grameen Bank pays 8.5 per cent annual interest on the balance.

The Emergency Fund

The money for this fund comes from a levy of 25 per cent on the interest on all loans to members, which is paid when the member makes the last repayment on a loan, usually fifty weeks after it was disbursed. The fund is used to provide life insurance for all members who have been clients of the Bank for year or more. Deceased members' families, or whoever they choose to nominate, receive 500 taka for the first full year they have been members, plus 200 taka for the second year plus 500 taka for every additional year. If there is not enough money in this fund, the balance can be borrowed from the Bank but must be repaid.

The Child Welfare Fund

One taka of each member's weekly savings of seven taka is given to this fund, which is used for building schools or pre-schools. By 1991 25 successful schools had been set up by the clients of the Bhawal Rajbari branch with help from this fund.

Members are also encouraged to save money in their own personal savings accounts; the Bank pays 8.5 per cent interest on these accounts, as it does on the balances in all the above funds. In October 1991 the Bhawal Rajbari branch held nearly half a million taka of its clients' money on their private savings accounts, which they could of course withdraw and use as they pleased.

The Grameen Bank had 781 branches at the end of 1990, and 134 more were added during 1991. The individual branches are not of course independent financial entities, but the Bank maintains records of their profitability and financial condition for management purposes. The operating results of the Bhawal Rajbari branch for 1990, and its financial condition at the end of the year, were very approximately as follows (figures in taka):

The Approximate Operating Results of the Branch for 1990

Income:		
Interest from loans		822,000
Rent paid by staff for accommodation		7,000
Total		829,000
Expenses:		
Interest on deposits and funds	233,000	
Interest on funds from H/O	135,000	
Salaries and bonus	253,000	
Travel	7,000	
Post, stationary and phone	15,000	
Depreciation	22,000	
Total	665,000	
Profit		164,000

Summarised Balance Sheet for the Branch on 31 December 1990

Assets		Liabilities	
Cash and bank	negligible	Member savings	
Loans and interest due	6,730,000	and funds	3,978,000
Salary advances	33,000	Owed to head office	3,633,000
Property and equipment	848,000		
Total	7,611,000		7,611,000

Loans for collective activities made up less than six per cent of the total loan portfolio of the Bhawal Rajbari branch. This was higher than for most branches, particularly the newer ones, and in the bank as a whole, more than 99 per cent of all loans were taken by individuals. Housing loans, for improving or constructing members' houses, made up almost a third of the amounts due. These averaged about 15,000 taka, and were repayable over ten years. Interest was charged at the special rate of five per cent. These loans were only available to people who had repaid three or more ordinary loans without any problem and who were members of successful groups which had been established for three years or more.

If any member of a group was in arrears with her repayments, no other member could take a loan. This rule meant that recoveries were maintained at a high level, and members would often help one another in times of difficulty in order to maintain their group's record. The Bhawal Rajbari branch claimed that 100 per cent of all loans were repaid eventually, although some settlements might be delayed because of ill health, crop failure or other causes.

Over 96 per cent of the clients of Grameen Bank in 1991 were women. This was partly the result of the bank's policy, because women's lack of access to financial services was an important aspect of their generally disadvantaged position in society. Experience had also shown that women used their earnings for the benefit of their families and they were more reliable payers than men; they also seemed able to work more effectively in groups.

The figures (in million taka) which follow summarise the operations and financial position of the Grameen Bank as a whole for 1991.

Summarised Accounts for year Ending 31 December 1991

Balance Sheet

Liabilities		Assets		
Capital	114	Cash		negligible
Reserves	9	Bank		67
Revolving Fund	1,278	Investments		1,450
Borrowings	1,876	General loans	1,775	
Members deposits	1,381	Housing loans	780	
Current Liabilities	183	Staff loans (Cycles)	21	
Total	4,841	Total loans	2,576	
		Less loss Provisions	25	
		Net loans		2,551
		Interest receivable	364	
		Less Provisions	35	
		Net interest receivable		329
		Fixed assets		344
		Other assets		99
		Loss for year		1
		Total		4,841

Profit and Loss Account for 1991

Income:	Interest on Loans	323
	Interest on investments	134
	Other Income	82
	Total	539
Expenses:	Interest on Deposits	69
	Interest on borrowings	50
	Salaries and Allowances	269
	Depreciation	17
	Training costs	60
	Other expenses	75
	Total	540
Net Loss:		1

The revolving fund was made up of money which had been given to Grameen Bank by foreign donors and was put into a fund from which the Bank borrowed at 2.5 per cent annual interest as required. This interest helped to maintain the value of the fund. The borrowings were from a variety of local and foreign institutions, at various generally subsidised rates of interest.

The Bhawal Rajbari branch continued to grow after 1991. The branch increased its number of clients by over 25 per cent, to 2,108 by the end of 1995. The value of loans outstanding increased by almost four times, and the value of clients' savings and other funds went up by three and a half times. The branch also maintained its profitability.

The Grameen Bank as a whole expanded at a rather faster rate, and the number of branches almost reached 1,100; there were over two million borrowers, and the proportion of women remained at about 96 per cent. The majority of the shares in the Bank was originally controlled by the government, but as it expanded the government chose not to subscribe the necessary capital to maintain its share. Members agreed to convert some part of their funds into equity, and by 1995 they controlled 92 per cent of the shares. The members elected their own representatives on the Board of Directors, and nine of the thirteen directors were village women, elected by their fellow group members.

The following summarised figures (in million taka) show the financial position and operations of Grameen Bank for 1995.

Summarised accounts for year ending 31 December 1995

Balance Sheet

Liabilities		Assets		
Capital	230	Cash		negligible
Reserves	90	Bank		430
Revolving fund	3,470	Investments		3,650
Borrowings	8,500	General loans	8,180	
Members deposits	340	Housing loans	3,480	
Group fund	3,030	Staff loans	300	
Provident fund	690	Total loans		11,960
Other funds	1,400	Less Provisions	860	
		Net loans		11,100
		Interest receivable	2,010	
		Less Provisions	270	
		Net interest, rec.		1,740
		Fixed assets		590
		Other assets		240
Total	17,750	Total		17,750

Approximate Profit and Loss account for 1995

Income:	Interest on heneral loans	1,680
	Interest on housing loans	280
	Interest on staff loans	20
	Interest on deposits	200
	Grants	80
	Other income	20
	Total	2,280
Expenses:	Interest on deposits	370
	Interest on borrowings	480
	Salaries and allowances	710
	Provisions	510
	Depreciation	20
	Training costs	50
	Other expenses	130
	Total	2,270
Net Profit:		10

In addition to the differences in the amounts, some other critical changes took place. Grameen Bank reduced its dependence on subsidised foreign funds by issuing bonds which were guaranteed by the government but were sold on the local money market at the prevailing rates of interest. The Bank has also started to diversify its own interests, and thus to widen its clients' opportunities for profitable activities. One subsidiary is involved in the design, procurement and export of handloom cloth, and is exporting fifteen million dollars worth each year, from 8,000 weavers. Grameen Communications, another subsidiary, is promoting a mobile telephone service which aims to provide self-employment opportunities and telephone services to village people. Numerous organisations in other countries are also 'replicating' the Grameen Bank model, and the Bank is actively involved in promoting and facilitating this process throughout the world.

(The exchange rate is approximately 50 taka = US$ 1.00.)

Comments and Issues

The Grameen Bank has been the subject of many books, articles and detailed evaluation studies. The scale of its achievement, and its impact on micro-finance and on development thinking in general, more than justifies the attention it has received. Any reader who wishes to find out more should refer to the extensive literature, and should above all try to participate in the excellent (and very reasonably priced) exposure programmes organised by the Bank. These programmes, which include extended visits to branches and clients, are obviously far more instructive than any written material or video presentation could ever be.

For the purposes of this case study collection, however, it may be worth posing certain questions. Most have been debated elsewhere, but every reader will have new insights, and the Grameen Bank will always be a source of inspiration, of ideas and lessons of what to do and perhaps also what not to do. The following questions of course cover only a small selection of the issues which the Bank's experience has highlighted:

1) The Grameen Bank is not self-sustaining, in the sense of covering all its costs, including the market cost of funds and a competitive return on its equity. Could it or should it be?

2) The two million borrowers from the Grameen Bank are engaged in a wide range of activities which are nevertheless limited by the skills and the market. Should the Bank not have tried before to introduce new skills and to develop new business opportunities to avoid market saturation and to increase clients' incomes?

3) Bangladesh is a very poor, very densely populated country with a fairly homogeneous society. How transferable is the Grameen Bank methodology to other circumstances?

4) The Grameen Bank has worked almost entirely in rural areas. Are its methods applicable in urban areas, of Bangladesh or anywhere else?

5) The Grameen Bank has been widely copied in Bangladesh, by NGOs. Could or should commercial banks, in Bangladesh or elsewhere, apply some part or the whole of the Grameen Bank method?

6) Clients' savings, either voluntary or 'forced' as part of the loan system, only contribute less than a third of the funds required for loans. Should Grameen Banks not offer more attractive and flexible savings facilities, both to serve clients better and to reduce dependence on other sources of funds?

7) Clients join the Grameen Bank 'system', and remain in it. Does this create undesirable dependence, or is it similar to anyone's long-term banking relationship?

8) The Grameen Bank system demands a great deal of staff time, and the time of its clients. This costs both parties money. Could or should it be made more efficient, and how?

CHAPTER 6

THE BANCO NACIONAL DE COMERCIO INTERIOR, MEXICO

The Banco Nacional del Pequeno Comercio (National Bank for Small Traders), or 'Banpeco' as it was usually called, was established by the Government of Mexico in 1943. Its task was to provide credit to small-scale retailers and wholesalers, in order that the many people engaged in these fields could benefit from institutional credit, and also in order to benefit the economy as a whole through a more efficient trading sector. In June 1992 the Bank's name was changed to Banco Nacional de Comercio Interior (BNCI), or National Bank for Domestic Commerce, in recognition of the extension of its credit activities beyond the field of small-scale traders, but its fundamental mission remained the same.

In 1988 it was estimated that almost one-and-a-half million people, or nearly twenty per cent of the total labour force, were employed in trading activities, and there were some 640,000 separate trading businesses, not including the probably far larger number of mobile vendors and others people who operated businesses along the streets, illegally or otherwise. There were a small number of chain stores and other large firms, but the vast majority were very small enterprises, providing work for around two people each, including their owners. By 1993 these figures had probably increased by around ten per cent; Banpeco was extending credit to some 85,000 separate establishments, or rather over ten per cent of the total market.

BNCI now has 135 branches, 27 of which are in the capital city, while the others are in smaller towns elsewhere in the country. The bank employs just over 3,000 people. In addition to the loans for small-scale traders which make up the bulk of its business, BNCI also lends money for the purchase of taxis and for the construction of new markets for traders who have no fixed locations. They also lend to large bakeries so that they in turn can make advances to small farmers for purchase of their grain.

The approximate balance sheet and profit and loss account for Banpeco for January 1993 and for the end of that month were as follows:

Banpeco (BNCI), Profit and Loss Account for January 1993

Interest Received		22,600,000*
Commissions and other sums received		4,200,000
Total income		26,800,000
Interest Paid	13,400,000	
Commissions, fees etc. paid	2,400,000	
Total direct costs	15,800,000	
Spread (Gross Margin)		11,000,000
Wages and Salaries	4,600,000	
Rents	900,000	
Promotion	100,000	
Depreciation and write-offs	3,900,000	
Local taxes etc.	300,000	
Other costs	1,600,000	
Total Expenses	11,400,000	
Operating Loss		400,000
Recoveries	2,600,000	
Total Profit		2,200,000
LESS Minority Interests		200,000
Net Profit		2,400,000

Banpeco (BNCI), Balance Sheet as at 31.12.1993

Assets		Liabilities	
Cash	9,100,000	Sight Deposits	119,000,000
Bank Balances	32,600,000	Savings Deposits	17,700,000
Fixed deposits	2,400,000	Other Deposits	58,600,000
Loans	603,000,000	Bank Drafts in circulation	150,000,000
Accounts Rec.	212,000,000	Time Deposits	31,600,000
Fixed Assets	62,600,000	Business Deposits	70,200,000
		Bankers Acceptances	155,400,000
		Official Deposits	39,200,000
		Bankers' deposits	17,900,000
		Mortgages	130,000,000
		Provisions	13,300,000
		Other Creditors	5,100,000
		Paid Up Capital	16,000,000
		Reserves	76,100,000
		Profit for 1992	19,200,000
		Profit Jan 1993	2,400,000
Total	921,700,000	Total	921,700,000

Like any bank which has to survive and grow from its own resources, Banpeco has always endeavoured to reduce its transaction costs, which

---

* All the figures in this case study are expressed, very approximately, in US $.

are the major reason why the other banks have not generally been willing to finance the smaller traders. One approach which has been followed from the early days of Banpeco's existence has been to appraise loans more on the basis of the market in which clients are tenants rather than on a client by client basis. The Bank has over time developed formulae for the amount of capital that each type of trader needs. The amount varies according to the size and location of the stall, which affects the volume of sales achieved, and the type of goods traded; some dried produce is purchased seasonally and lasts for many months, so that large stocks can be held, while fresh fruit and vegetables have to be re-purchased daily. The credit which is offered varies accordingly. Loans to these public market stallholders can also be secured against the right to occupy the particular stall, which reduces the risk of loss.

Banpeco has also reduced appraisal costs by changing from term-lending to a system of credit lines, which is similar to overdrafts. Each business is allowed a certain maximum credit, and the owner can draw up to this amount as he wishes. Interest is calculated daily on the amount outstanding, and is charged to the accounts monthly. The rate of interest is 34 per cent per year, which is about 4 per cent higher than the rate charged to larger commercial borrowers by other banks; when a client's account is in credit, interest is credited by Banpeco at an annual rate of eight per cent.

Another more recent approach to reducing branch transaction costs is by using a credit card system and automatic cash dispensers. Clients are asked to clear their overdrafts and are then given a credit card which can be used to withdraw cash up to their credit limit from the numerous cash-dispensing machines which have been installed by many banks, particularly in Mexico City. The machines can also receive cash, so that clients can pay into their accounts through them as well, and although Banpeco pays a fee of 3 per cent of each transaction to the bank which owns the machine this is less expensive than the cost per transaction over the counter at a branch.

In order to encourage its customers to change over to credit card banking Banpeco has reduced the annual interest rate charged on these accounts to 29 per cent. Although this is 5 per cent lower than the rate charged for the same facility when it is provided across the counter by bank staff, many customers are reluctant to change over. This may be because they prefer personal contact, or it may be that they are nervous about having to close the manual account before opening the card account, since they fear that their facility may not be extended. In any case, to date only about 18,000 clients have made the change.

Banpeco pays interest of between 12 per cent and 15 per cent on deposit accounts, depending on the term, and 8 per cent on passbook savings accounts. Clients used to be required to accumulate savings to a level of 10 per cent of their proposed credit line as a condition of borrowing, and to retain this amount, but some traders complained that this was unfair in that they had better uses for their money. Banpeco therefore dropped this requirement, and clients are no longer compelled to save before being allowed to borrow, nor are they required to have savings accounts.

In its early years the Bank based its branches actually in stalls in the public markets themselves, because this was relatively inexpensive and very convenient for their clients. This practice has since been discontinued, because the stall spaces were very small, security was difficult, and an increasing number of clients were not operating within the market, but were occupying shops outside. They were reluctant to do their banking in the market but the market stall tenants did not mind crossing the street to a bank branch outside.

The Bank also tried to extend credit to the many thousands of very small-scale traders who operated their businesses in temporary or mobile stalls on pavements and in the streets. This was not successful; there was a substantial demand, but the repayment record was very bad, because the Bank did not have the right to seize the clients' market stall as a threat against default; although this right is hardly ever exercised, it is a powerful motivator.

BNCI management now feels that the best way to help these very small traders is not to lend them money direct, but to help them by financing new market buildings, which may be promoted by municipal authorities, by traders' associations or by private developers.

The Merced Branch of BNCI is situated across the street from the central vegetable market; this is the largest retail and wholesale market in Mexico city, and there are over 4,000 stall holders selling vegetables alone.

The main business of the branch is with stall holders in the market; these traders own the right of occupancy of their stalls, subject to regular payment of their very modest rents, and Banpeco has an agreement with the market administration that if a customer defaults on a loan the bank has the right to seize and dispose of the stall in order to recover the amount due. The Banpeco branch has only once exercised this right in the last few years; their field staff visit clients who are in arrears as soon as the position becomes evident, and these clients usually pay after some discussion and simple advice. Those who do not wish to continue their businesses can sell their stalls, and the proceeds are always sufficient to pay back any outstanding instalments to BNCI.

The procedure for extending credit is more or less the same at any branch; the bank's staff does a detailed study of the market, assessing a sample of traders in each category of goods in order to assess the capital requirements. Individual traders then apply to the branch. There are 20 staff working at the Merced branch and one of the three field workers briefly visits the client at his or her stall in order to check that it falls more or less into the previously calculated norms. If all is well the account is opened with a credit limit up to the prescribed amount. The limit can be increased either because of inflation or when the trader can show that his business has increased so that he needs a larger facility.

The Merced branch is at the end of February 1993 extending credit to 2,309 clients; the various categories are as follows:

Stallholders in the Central Market, personal customers	1,459
Stallholders in the Central Market, card credit lines	633
Regular shopkeepers, personal customers	85
Regular shopkeepers, card credit lines	16
Regular credit cardholders	106
Non-performing accounts	10

About half the clients are women, and many of the businesses are run by husband and wife teams. The actual number of borrowers, as opposed to accounts, is somewhat smaller than the above figures suggest, because some traders hold several stalls in the names of relatives and others who do not themselves work in the market, and they have separate credit lines in the name of each stall. This is technically illegal, but it is nevertheless common practice. The average loan is about $1300, but the 2,000 market stall holders are mostly borrowing a little over $300 each; the higher average is caused by a few larger accounts held by wholesale traders operating outside the market.

The Merced branch is one of four in the Number Two Metropolitan Area; the area office is located in the same building as the branch, but the branch manager has a reasonable degree of lending discretion up to a certain limit; an approximate balance sheet for 31.12.92 and profit and loss account for the branch for December 1992 are as follows:

Balance Sheet

Assets		Liabilities	
Cash	17,000	Customer Savings and Deposits	4,520,000
Current loans	3,026,000		
Overdue loans	124,000		
Equipment	5,000		
Deposit to HQ	1,348,000		
Total	4,520,000	Total	4,520,000

Profit and Loss Account for December 1 to 31, 1992	
Interest on current loans	88,000
Interest paid on H/O deposit	20,000
Other interest	15,000
Commissions	10,000
Other income	18,000
Total income	151,000
Interest paid on deposits	58,000
Net income	93,000
Operating costs	23,000
Administrative costs	41,000
Depreciation	5,000
Total costs	69,000
Net profit	24,000

Jimenes and his wife run a retail and wholesale dried-fish product business at stall 19 in the market; they also have a storage unit outside the market for their wholesale business. They have a $ 13,000 credit line with BNCI, which has been increased from the $ 3,000 limit with which they started six years ago. They estimate that they clear a profit of about $ 1,300 a month from their sales of about $ 5,000. Their costs apart from the cost of goods and their own labour are negligible; rent is about $ 40 a month, and their suppliers and customers arrange for the transport of their own goods.

They are not sure what rate of interest is charged on their credit line, and their loan amount outstanding normally fluctuates between around $ 5,000 and $ 14,000 depending on the season and the time of the month. They hold about $ 50,000 worth of goods in stock, and the lease of the stall is worth about $ 15,000 although they paid very little for it when they first occupied it some years ago. The balance of the capital is provided from their own initial investment and their subsequent re-investment of profits.

Samvel Salina is a smaller customer, with a credit line of about $ 1,000. He and his wife and one employee run a fresh vegetable stall, and their sales are about $ 10,000 a month. They hold stock worth about $ 1,500, and they estimate that their gross margin is about $ 2,000 a month. Samvel and his wife each draw about $ 700 a month salary; they pay their worker $ 200 a month, plus food. Their credit from BNCI varies between zero and $ 2,000, although the average is about $ 1,000. Samvel is not sure whether BNCI charges them 3 per cent interest per month or per year, but he is happy with the relationship.

Comments and Questions

This Bank was established in 1943, but it shares many of the characteristics of the so-called 'new generation' micro-finance institutions. Mexico is also far less poor than many of the less developed countries where some of the other systems described in these case studies are operating. The scale of the businesses operated by the BNCI clients, and the amounts of their loans, as well as the use of modern banking technology such as automatic tellers, are perhaps closer to the United States or Europe than to South Asia or East Africa. When the Bank started, however, the economic scale and conditions of its clients were very similar to those in many poorer countries today. Newer institutions can learn from the BNCI experience.

The following issues, among others, merit consideration:

1) The Merced branch of BNCI, and the Bank as a whole, are taking more from their customers in deposits and other savings instruments than they are giving in loans. Is this an appropriate balance for a finance institution whose objective is to assist poor people ?

2) BNCI offers a full banking service to its clients, just like any other bank. Should micro-finance institutions try to compete with full service commercial banks in this way, or should they confine their products to those which are particularly needed by their client group ?

3) The BNCI system of loan appraisal and collateral has evolved in response to the particular circumstances of market traders who operate from fixed locations in organised urban markets. What aspects of the system might be applicable to different types of clients, particularly smaller traders who are not fortunate enough to have a place in the main markets ?

4) BNCI has moved from fixed-term loans to cash credit limits, or overdrafts. Is this not a more convenient and economical way of providing working capital to micro-businesses, and what prevents more micro-finance institutions from adopting the same policy ?

5) Automatic teller machines are becoming available in most countries, and are spreading from wealthy down-town centres to areas such as market districts. How can micro-finance institutions make use of them, and how can they persuade their clients to accept this form of banking ?

6) BNCI failed to extend its services to smaller traders outside the city markets. Should they try again, and how could they avoid the problems they experienced in their first attempt ?

7) BNCI serves one particular market segment. Should micro-finance institutions focus their services in this way, or should they try to reach a broader range of types of client ?

8) The BNCI experience suggests that quite significant differences in interest rates are not important, even to clients who are borrowing several thousand dollars. For what types of businesses, and what types of loans, do interest rates become important determinants of clients' choice of lenders ?

9) Ever since its establishment, BNCI has financed its growth through re-investment of profits and accessing finance from its clients and others at market rates. Is it reasonable to expect micro-finance institutions to survive and grow entirely from their own resources, after the injection of initial equity capital, so long as the owners of this capital do not demand any dividends ?

CHAPTER 7

THE GAZARIA BRANCH, BRAC, BANGLADESH

Gazaria is an island of about 60 square km. It lies 40 km to the South East of Dhaka, the capital of Bangladesh. The main road to the city of Chittagong runs across the island, but until the new 'Japanese Friendship Bridge' was opened in 1991, Gazaria could only be reached by a one-hour ferry journey. About 112,000 people live on Gazaria. Their main source of income is fishing, with some rice cultivation in summer and wheat and potatoes in winter. It is one of the poorest parts of Bangladesh, and this was why a branch of the Bangladesh Rural Advancement Committee (BRAC) was established there in 1983.

BRAC was formed in February 1972, immediately after Bangladesh became independent. It started as a group of like-minded people who wanted to undertake short-term relief for refugees, but they soon realised that permanent solutions to rural poverty could only be achieved if the people were able to mobilise, manage and control local and external resources by themselves.

BRAC started its development work in the field of child health, and then expanded into primary education, and training. It soon became clear that the village people could never take control over their own lives if they remained dependent on village moneylenders. The BRAC savings and credit programme was therefore started in 1979. Like all the BRAC programmes, this was implemented with and through village organisations. By 1992 there were 147 branches of BRAC; each had its own savings and credit programme, organised on the same lines.

By 1992 the Gazaria branch had set up a total of 37 men's village organisation (VOs) and 92 for women, with an average membership of fifty people in each. The 129 VOs had a total membership of 6450 people, and 4,100 of them were making use of the BRAC loan facility. They were using their loans for a wide variety of trading and other small-scale businesses, and they also had a few collective ventures such as shallow tube wells.

There were also 77 BRAC-sponsored primary schools in Gazaria, each with about 30 children, and the BRAC branch was working in 51 of the

65 villages in the island. The other 14 villages were inaccessible from the branch office and the norm for BRAC offices was in any case a maximum of about 50 villages and 120 VOs; the Gazaria branch was operating at well over its capacity.

BRAC's management had a clear strategy for the savings and credit operation. They wanted to continue and expand the rate of new branch formation, which was currently running at about twenty branches a year, but they wanted at the same time to transfer the well-established savings and credit operations, such as that in Gazaria, to a new and self-sustaining operation, to be known as BRAC Bank. This could only be done if the operation was self-sustaining, and Mohamed Jahangir, the manager of the Gazaria BRAC office, saw his task quite clearly. He had to make the savings and credit operations of the branch into a profitable enterprise.

The branch had a total staff of 23 people. These included the Manager, Mohamed Jahangir, four rural development programme organisers, thirteen village development workers, an accountant and four education programme organisers. The branch occupied a half-acre site near the middle of the island, with a small office block and accommodation for the manager and the four programme organisers. The other staff lived in the nearby village.

The banking operation was managed by Mohamed Jahangir, working through two of the four programme organisers who specialised in savings and credit, and the thirteen village development workers. One of the other programme organisers was responsible for helping members with their enterprises. He was skilled in some activities himself, and he could also call on specialist BRAC services and supplies such as poultry vaccines or animal husbandry advisers. The other non-banking organiser specialised in institutional development for the 129 VOs, with particular emphasis on new groups and those where problems occurred.

While the main activity of the VOs was credit, and this was the reason most members joined, they had to go through a rather lengthy preparation process before they were eligible for a loan. The VOs had to meet every week, and each member had to save a minimum of two taka per week. They also had to complete a thirty-day training course, of two hours a day. This was designed to help the members, and in particular the women, to understand their own position and to realise that by working together they could redress many of the social, political and economic injustices from which they suffered. This was relevant for all the members, because they were all poor. Only people with less than half an acre of land, and who had to work for others as day labourers for at least one hundred days a year in order to survive, were allowed to join.

The VO members also learned some basic health and sanitary rules, and they had to commit to memory a list of seventeen rules which they had to recite at the beginning of every weekly meeting. The training also included an introduction to the BRAC systems which they would have to follow. Men had to have been VO members for at least six months before they could take a loan, while women were allowed to borrow after three months. This was because BRAC wanted particularly to assist women, the most disadvantaged members of Bangladesh society, and also because women had proved to be more reliable borrowers.

Most of the men's VO meetings took place at 6.30 am and the women's at 8.30 am. This not only fitted in with their respective household and farming tasks, but it also meant that a development worker could be present at every meeting. The members met at the same time and place every week, usually in an open space in the middle of the village or in a member's house if it was raining.

The members were organised into smaller sub-groups of around five members each. They sat on the ground for their meetings in a regular pattern. The sub-group leaders made up the front row, and their respective members sat behind them. This made it easy to see at once if everybody was present, and it also made the financial transactions much easier to control.

The meetings started with a roll call. After this, each member passed her savings forward, together with her passbook, to her group leader in the front row. The development worker then passed along the row, checking the money and entering and signing the payments in each passbook. The members then passed forward their loan repayments, which were also checked and signed for by the development worker. The majority of loans were for one year, with 52 payments of the same amount, due weekly. This meant that most members had a repayment to make each week. Interest was charged at 20 per cent, calculated on the declining balance.

The sub-group leaders then presented verbally any loan applications which members of their group wished to put forward. They did this verbally, because most of the members were illiterate, particularly the women who made up the majority of the organisations. The sub-group leaders had previously discussed and agreed the applications with the prospective borrowers and other members of their group. Only two or three members of each subgroup were allowed to have outstanding loans at any one time, and they were all responsible for each others' repayments, so every members took an active interest in her fellow-members' applications and repayments.

The first loan could not exceed 3,000 taka, the maximum for the second loan was 5,000 taka, and the third and all subsequent loans could not exceed 7,000 taka. Members were allowed to have a maximum of two loans outstanding at the same time.

If the majority of all the VO members, the VO chairperson and the development worker agreed, the worker would then make a note of the applicant's name, the amount and the proposed purpose of the loan, and would take them to the branch manager. If the manager agreed the worker would then prepare a simple loan application form. This had to be signed by the applicant, the sub-group leader and the VO chairperson. The branch manager would then submit the collected loan application forms to his Regional Manager. Mohamed Jahangir's Regional Manager could veto loans which he had approved, although he very rarely did, but he was not allowed to over-rule the branch manager's own veto.

When the loan was approved, the applicant could then collect the money from the branch office. This was the only time a member ever had to go to the office, since all savings and repayments were made at the weekly VO meetings. The maximum time between the first application and disbursement of the cash was fifteen days.

Ten per cent was automatically deducted from all loans at the time of disbursement. Five per cent was deposited in the member's own personal savings account, four per cent was put in a trust fund which could be used for community projects such as schools, and one per cent was taken as a life insurance premium. This guaranteed the family of every member a lump sum payment of 5,000 taka in case of death.

BRAC classified the outstanding loan balances into three categories for the purpose of monitoring recoveries. Current balances were those where the final repayment date, usually 52 weeks from disbursement, had not been reached, regardless of how up-to-date repayments were within that period. Late balances were those which had gone beyond the 52 week deadline, and had therefore been rescheduled by agreement with the branch manager. Overdue balances were those rescheduled amounts which had themselves not been paid by the new dates which had been agreed.

The Gazaria branch had a slightly better repayment record than the average for the other 146 BRAC branches; the comparative figures in 1992 were as follows (given as percentages of the amount owing):

	Gazaria Branch	All BRAC branches
Current balances	94	90
Late balances	2	7
Overdue balances	4	3

BRAC had a policy of not writing off old overdue amounts, since most were eventually recovered. Cases had occurred when loans which were many years overdue had been repaid, by relatives, by other VO members or by the borrower herself, and BRAC did not want in any way to reduce this sense of responsibility. The VOs were legally responsible for the repayment of all their members' loans, since their elected leaders had approved them and all the members had agreed to accept the responsibility as a condition of membership. BRAC therefore had a legal right to seize a VO's accumulated savings in case of default, this step had actually never been taken.

What actually happened was that the other members of a subgroup, or of the VO if the sub-group failed, would persuade defaulting members to pay. They would use social pressure or the threat of seizing their possessions, or, very rarely, they would hire a lawyer to threaten legal action, independently of BRAC itself. If the members were agreed that the default was quite outside the control of the member, because of death, serious illness or some other calamity, they would sometimes pay from their own cash or savings, or would draw money from their VO trust fund.

The 13 development workers at the Gazaria branch each had responsibility for about ten VOs, with an average loan portfolio of over 600,000 taka each. The members of some VOs in better-off areas than Gazaria were able to use more money, and they had loans of over 100,000 taka per group. This meant that their development workers were responsible for a portfolio of over a million taka.

The development workers were paid a salary of about 2,000 taka a month. This was about twice the minimum wage for unskilled workers, and was more or less the same as the earnings of people of similar qualifications doing similar work in the government, but BRAC's management were anxious to motivate them to improve the quality of their work. They would also have to work very hard to achieve the efficiency and high loan recovery rates which were essential if the new BRAC bank was to be a success.

Management therefore decided to try out an incentive payment system for the development workers, based on their performance in the field. It was obviously important that they should not be motivated to build loan volume without any regard for quality, and there were many other possible difficulties, particularly as none of the other BRAC staff were paid on an incentive basis.

The trial scheme was as follows:

Development workers were to receive a bonus of one per cent of all on-time collections of current loans, or of late loans collected as rescheduled, provided that collections during the month were 98 per cent of what was scheduled.

If collections were 100 per cent of what was scheduled, the bonus was to be one-and-a-half per cent of collections.

In addition, they were to receive two per cent of any excess over whatever target for collections of overdues was set by the branch manager, if he chose to set such a target.

Management estimated that the maximum likely commission would be about 600 taka a month, or a 30 per cent increase in basic salary. In order to assess its likely impact, they introduced the scheme for a trial period in a small number of branches, including Gazaria.

After one month, three of the thirteen development workers had earned a bonus of about 250 taka each, and the other ten had earned no bonus at all. Some of the other trial branches had similar experiences, while in others nobody earned a bonus. Some of the staff were discouraged, because they were responsible for weaker VOs and it appeared unlikely that they could ever reach the 98 per cent minimum on-time repayment rate. In many cases they had taken over these weak VOs from development workers who had left or been transferred, and they felt it was unfair that they should be penalised for having to work with difficult groups.

Management had to decide whether to abandon the experiment, or extend the scheme, as it was or after some modification and further testing, to all the well-established BRAC offices. They realised that there were many other possible problems as well as the ones which had already been identified in Gazaria and elsewhere, and they also knew it would be very difficult to withdraw such a scheme once it hd been introduced throughout the organisation.

Mohamed Jahangir had to advise management on this issue, but his major concern was to ensure that the Gazaria branch was one of the first to be genuinely self-sustaining, so that it could justify its transfer to the new BRAC Bank.

In November 1992 the financial position of the branch was approximately as follows (all figures are in taka):

Assets		Liabilities	
Cash/bank	65,000	Members' savings	3,800,000
Loans	8,100,000	VO Trust funds	1,000,000
Bicycles/office eqpt	102,000	Balance funds	
Land and building	1,135,000	from head office	4,602,000
Total	9,402,000	Total	9,402,000

The land was actually worth about ten times its original purchase price, but it was kept in the books at its original value. The BRAC branch maintained a current account at the local branch of the Sonali Bank, one of the nationalised commercial banks which had offices on Gazaria, and BRAC had negotiated an overdraft facility of up to 400,000 taka from that bank which could be used when necessary, at the normal commercial interest rate of 16 per cent.

No internal charge was made on the branches for the funds from head office, which mainly came from international donors, but BRAC planned to introduce a 6 per cent annual interest charge on these funds in the near future, in order to cover its own head office costs.

The approximate monthly operating revenues and costs for the savings and credit operations of the BRAC Gazaria branch in November 1992 were as follows (all figures are in taka):

Revenue:		
Loan interest		125,000
Late payment penalties		1,000
Total income		126,000
Costs:		
Savings interest at 9 per cent	34,000	
Manager's salary	5,000	
Programme organisers, 2 at 3,500 taka	7,000	
Development workers, 13 at 2,000 taka	26,000	
Accountant salary	2,500	
Support staff	5,000	
Staff benefits at 25 per cent of salaries	13,000	
Staff travel, maintenance, stationery,	10,500	
Depreciation	10,000	
Total costs		113,000
Surplus		13,000

These figures excluded the costs of the staff who were not employed in the savings and credit operation, and were the best estimates of its actual costs. BRAC had already applied for official registration of the proposed Bank, and this was expected to be finalised in 1993 or 1994, but Mohamed Jahangir's branch was already effectively operating as a local bank. The members' savings, and the loans, were growing at an annual rate of about 20 per cent. Inflation was running at about 10 per cent per year, so this meant that the real rate of growth was about 10 per cent annually.

Mohamed Jahangir's first target was to cover the cost of the funds being used, at the admittedly subsidised rate of 6 per cent for money 'borrowed' from head office. Like everyone else, however, Mohamed Jahangir did not want to rely on donor assistance for ever. He wanted the Gazaria branch to be able in due course to cover the real cost of its funds, and to be able in due course to contribute to the accumulation of the new capital which BRAC Bank would need if it was ever to become a genuinely self-sustaining bank for the poor.

(The exchange rate is approximately 50 taka = US$ 1.00.)

Comments and Questions

The BRAC system described in this case is clearly similar to that used by the Bhawal Rajbari branch of the Grameen Bank, but there are a number of important differences. These relate to the origins, the present activities and some operating details of the two institutions. BRAC has in general learned from and followed the Grameen Bank methods, rather than the reverse, but the differences say a great deal about the organisation culture of the two organisations, and about the way in which they are evolving.

The following questions may be relevant, among others:

1) BRAC was originally a social welfare organisation, and its financial operation was evolved as a result of experience in other fields. How are these different origins reflected in the present financial system ?

2) BRAC's banking clients also receive other non-banking services from BRAC. Should these services be provided by the same organisation that provides savings and credit, or should they be separated ?

3) BRAC's VO members have to make substantial 'forced savings', which very significantly increase the effective cost of their loans. Is it right to impose such requirements on poor people, who have no alternative source of financial services ?

4) How useful is the BRAC system of classifying loan balances for the purpose of monitoring recoveries ? How might it be improved ?

5) Should BRAC extend, modify or drop the proposed incentive payment system ? Should micro-finance loan staff generally be paid on results or on a flat basis ?

6) How can the Gazaria branch manager bring his branch to break-even point when the new 6 per cent charge on head office funds is imposed ?

7) Is BRAC right to impose a notional charge of 6 per cent on funds which it received interest free ?

8) Is the proposed 6 per cent charge sufficient ? If not, how much should be charged, and how could the Gazaria branch cover whatever charge is appropriate ?

CHAPTER 8

THE OMDURMAN PRODUCTIVE FAMILIES BRANCH OF THE SUDAN-ISLAMIC BANK

Sharia Financial Systems

Muhammad was a successful trader for many years before he became a Prophet, and capital for his ventures was provided on a profit or loss sharing basis by a wealthy widow, Khadijah, who later became his wife. She shared not only in the financing but also in the management of the business, and she might even be considered as the first documented woman entrepreneur.

Trade, with its associated risks, was fundamental to the economy of Arabia, since communities tended not to be self-sufficient and they depended on the movement of goods over large distances, in difficult and dangerous terrain, which required substantial risk capital. The Koran indeed commends trade (Surah 2, verse 198), and defines the poor (ibid., verse 273) as those who need alms because they 'cannot travel in the land for trade'.

The Koran also deals with a number of economic and financial issues. Money is seen not as the property of individuals, nor or of the state, but as belonging to the community at large. Idle funds should be subject to heavy taxes for the benefit of the poor, so that people are encouraged to put their money to work by investing it in productive ventures, and the rules for inheritance are designed to preserve wealth within the wider family and to prevent concentration in too few hands.

The Koran gives very detailed guidance as to the necessity for written business contracts, duly witnessed, (Surah 2, verse 282) and it also specifically prohibits usury, in several different contexts (see for example Surah 2, verse 275, Surah 3, verse 130, and Surah 30, verse 39).

There are a number of reasons why usury, or 'riba', is forbidden. It is said to be wrong because the lender is seen merely to be exploiting other people's needs, since he does not share the work or the risk, but gains his reward nevertheless, and the setting of fixed interest rates is seen as implying ability to forecast the future. Because the future is not under our control, this implication is perceived as being wrong.

Opinions differ, as they do in other contexts, as to whether "usury' refers to excessive interest charges, or to the very principle of lending money for a fixed and certain return. Within Islam there are two views on this, which have been characterised as the 'modernist' and the 'conservative' views. According to the modernist view, reasonable interest charges are permitted, whereas the conservative view holds that any kind of fixed interest is wrong. In any case, although fixed interest banking is practised in many Islamic countries, there is also a complete alternative system, which conforms to Sharia law, and which has recently been applied with some success to small enterprise lending.

There are several forms of Sharia credit; the most widely used is known as Murabaha. Under this system, the client specifies the asset for which he needs finance, and the banker then purchases it and resells it at an agreed profit to the client. The client repays the banker in agreed instalments, over time, and the profit compensates the banker for the loss of use of the money and the risk of non-repayment. There is no specific interest charge, but in effect Murabaha is clearly little different from an interest-bearing loan.

Musharaka Partnerships

The other form of Islamic investment is what is called Musharaka, or partnership credit, which is very close to what in other financial contexts is known as venture capital. Under this system, the banker contributes a certain proportion of the investment required for a given venture, and he agrees with the entrepreneur as to the distribution of the profits. They agree on the wage, if any, to which the entrepreneur will be entitled as a cost of the venture, to be deducted from the revenue along with the other expenses, and they agree that a certain share of the profits, usually between 20 per cent and 30 per cent, will be allocated to the entrepreneur for his management, or entrepreneurship. The balance of the profit is then shared in the same proportion as the original investment.

This form of partnership is ideally suited for single time-bound ventures, such as investments in trading expeditions like those which Muhammad undertook in partnership with the widow Khadijah, or in seasonal crops, which can be totally liquidated when they are completed. In such cases the banker may contribute all the working capital, including the farmer's wages, while the farmer contributes the use of his land and the depreciation of any equipment that is used.

Musharaka can also be adopted for continuing businesses. The partners agree on the share of the profits to be allocated to the entrepreneur for his management, and the balance is shared in the same proportion as their respective investments. The entrepreneur also agrees to buy out the banking partner over an agreed period, by paying a certain per centage of the original investment each year, and the banker receives a smaller proportion of the profits each year, as his share decreases.

There are a number of variants of both Murabaha and Musharaka investment, but the principles are fundamentally the same. Murabaha is close to the Western concept of hire purchase, which is of course a very important source of capital for fixed asset purchases by small business people, but Musharaka represents something quite new; the methodology and spirit of venture capital are applied by mainstream commercial bankers for the benefit of small enterprises.

Since the amount of money recovered by each partner is based on a proportion of the profits actually earned, and is not fixed in monetary terms when the agreement is made, it is automatically adjusted for inflation. This does not apply to the repayments of the banker's initial investments in declining partnerships, but in small enterprises at any rate the annual profits are usually well in excess of the original investment, so that this compensates for the lack of inflation indexing. If there are no profits to share, the banker gets nothing, and the operating partner is therefore not burdened with a debt in case of failure. If the risks are correctly calculated by the banker, his losses from failures will be met by his share of the profits earned by successful enterprises.

Sharia Finance in Sudan

Sudan provides one of the world's harshest testing grounds for any form of economic initiative. The general economic performance has been among the worst in the world. GNP per head declined by 22 per cent in real terms between 1966 and 1986, the richest 10 per cent of the population increased their share of national income from 32 per cent to 36 per cent, and the share of the poorest 40 per cent declined from 16 per cent to 12 per cent over a ten-year period. Inflation ran at an annual average rate of 160 per cent in the 1980s; current performance is if anything worse.

Sudan is also a country in which Islamic law, or Sharia, has come to be enforced in many fields, so that there is a strong incentive for banks to adopt Islamic banking methods. This is not only politically expedient, but it is also good marketing, since many of the people, and particularly the poor, adhere strictly to Sharia themselves. They are reluctant to borrow money, or to deposit their savings, on 'Western' interest-based terms.

The two major sectoral development banks, the Industrial Bank of Sudan and the Agricultural Bank of Sudan, have provided very little finance for smaller enterprises or farmers, and they have relied mainly on 'administrative charges' as a replacement for interest. A relatively small number of large farmers and industrialists have benefited from large loans of this kind which have often been invested in capital-intensive imported technology; the banks themselves have in recent years become largely inactive because of accumulated losses and inflation.

Most commercial banks, such as the Sudanese Savings Bank, have confined their assistance to smaller enterprises, which has been very limited in any case, to Murabaha, or purchase and re-sale operations, because this form of banking is relatively simple and understandable to their staff, who have mainly been trained in Western banking methods. Since the bank holds a lien over the asset until it is paid for, it appears relatively secure.

The Sudanese Islamic Bank

One exception, however, has been the Sudanese Islamic Bank (SIB). This is one of the largest commercial banks in Sudan with twenty million dollars paid up capital, 72 per cent of which is locally owned. This organisation, as its name implies, has always operated on Islamic principles; their earlier operations with smaller enterprises were mainly carried out on the basis of Murabaha, or purchase and resale. In 1987, for instance, the bank collaborated with the Dutch government in the supply of 150,000 chicks to one thousand small farmers; these were bought by the bank, and re-sold at a profit which covered the bank's transaction costs.

The SIB has in recent years been moving more towards partnership financing, partly because of the continuing high inflation rate in Sudan. The proportion of their investments which were made on the basis of Musharaka rose from 43 per cent in 1986 to 61 per cent in 1987, and an increasing proportion of this investment is being directed towards smaller enterprises. This is in marked contrast to other Islamic banks; in Iran, for instance, partnership investments only made up 31 per cent of the total disbursements made by the banks in 1986, and the proportion was more or less unchanged from the previous year.

Musharaka is ideal for financing seasonal agriculture. In a typical case, the bank entered into a partnership with 14 farmers in Karari, near Khartoum, to grow potatoes. The bank provided 71 per cent of the finance, much of it in kind through the use of tractors and pumps, and the cost of land clearance and inputs, while the farmers provided the balance of 29 per cent of the investment. It was agreed in this case that the farmers would receive 75 per cent of the final profits, in recognition of their management input and the use of their land, while 25 per cent of the profit would go to the SIB. In the event the bank earned a nominal return of 53 per cent on its investment, on an annualised basis, while the farmers earned 494 per cent on their contribution.

Sudan is a shortage economy, where access to inputs such as those provided by the SIB in this case is very difficult for individual farmers or others. The bank's contribution in kind, which may be made through its own subsidiary farm contracting business, is thus particularly valuable. It might otherwise be impossible for the farmers to obtain these resources even if they did have the money. The SIB is also able through its involvement in the actual operation to maintain contact, and thus to have some idea of the final yield and the profit. Like any partnership, Musharaka depends on a degree of trust between the partners, but such contact is nevertheless valuable.

The SIB can also finance post-harvest storage and marketing of crops, under separate Musharaka partnerships. In the case of sorghum, for instance, the SIB pays the farmer 50 per cent of the usually very low market price at the time of harvest. The farmer stores the whole crop, under the supervision of the bank, and when it is sold at an agreed date for a higher price the bank first recovers the down payment it made to the farmer. The farmer then receives 50 per cent of the net profit for his management, and the balance remaining is split equally between the bank and the farmer.

This provides a reasonable profit to the bank, and the combined arrangement enables the farmer to retain a far higher proportion of the value of his crop than he received under the traditional informal 'shail' system, whereby private traders provide an advance at planting time in return for the right to purchase the whole crop at harvest, for a price even lower than the market rate at that time.

On-going small enterprises, as opposed to seasonal farming or trading ventures, usually need some element of fixed capital, and in these cases Musharaka partnerships can include a prior agreement on a diminishing partnership as previously described. The operating partner buys out the bank's share over an agreed period of say five years, for the face value of original investment; the balance of the profits of the business is shared in proportion to the reduced share of ownership. When the full amount of the fixed capital has been repaid, the operating partner retains all the profit and has no further obligation to the bank.

This approach also has potential for small-scale non-farm enterprises, although the variety of different types of activity involved is likely to prevent the bank from being actually involved in the business as it is with some agricultural ventures. In 1992 the Bank established a special branch in one of the poorer areas of Omdurman, the original capital of Sudan which is in fact much larger than Khartoum, the adjacent colonial capital on the other side of the River Nile. The population of Omdurman has been enormously increased in recent years by the influx of refugees from internal and foreign warfare, and by people who have left rural areas because of long periods of drought.

This first specialist branch, which is known as 'The Productive Families Branch', has been opened because the Bank wishes to serve these people, in order both to reach a new and profitable market and to fulfil its social obligations.

The Omdurman branch was established in January 1992; after one year its financial position was approximately as follows (the figures are expressed in US dollars converted at the rate prevailing in January 1993; any form of conversion involves a compromise between totally unrealistic 'official' rates and widely varying unofficial figures):

Assets		Liabilities	
Partnership investments	54,000	Customer deposits	1,76,000
Other investments	56,000	Bank's original investment	16,000
Furniture and banking equipment	16,000		
Stocks of machinery	65,000		
Cash	1,000		
Total	1,92,000	Total	1,92,000

The 'other investments' are outstanding Murabaha, or purchase and resale, debts. Because the staff were familiar with this form of finance, much of the early investment was made on this basis, but because of the high and unpredictable level of inflation, the Bank is now focussing on Musharaka risk sharing partnerships, and few further purchase and resale investments are being made.

The Bank intends this branch to be self-sustaining not only in terms of earnings but also in terms of matching its deposits with investments, or credits; the branch has therefore invested the surplus deposits in sewing machines and other similar items of capital equipment which its clients use. These will be used in future partnerships, and the bank is protecting itself and its clients from inflation by holding its assets in readily marketable equipment rather than in cash or other financial instruments.

The operations of the branch over its first year can be summarised as follows (figures in US dollars):

Income from investments		32,000
Wages and salaries	9,600	
Rent	2,400	
Depreciation	9,880	
Total		21,880
Total profit of branch		10,120
80 per cent payable to depositors		8,096
20 per cent retained by Bank		2,024

The Bank actually invests its own share of the branch's profits in welfare services in the community, such as health and education, but this is in the nature of an initial goodwill gesture; the profits on the Bank's original investment in the branch are considered more than adequate, particularly in the first year of operation, and it is planned to extend the experiment more widely in the near future.

At the beginning of 1993 the branch was financing about 400 people. Two hundred and sixty of them were Musharaka investment partners, while the remainder were paying off Murabaha debts, and 80 per cent of them were women. The bank had invested an average of around $150 in each venture. Most of these partners were also depositors, and there were also two hundred additional depositors who were not at that time using the bank as a source of finance.

The partners are involved in a typically wide range of petty urban enterprises; about sixty of them are tailors, and others are manufacturing processed foodstuffs, soap, shoes, school chalk, cheese and wood and metal furniture. Yet others are raising goats or poultry, and many other partners are involved in petty retail trade.

During the first year there were no defaults. This does not mean, of course, that every business has been a successful investment; since payments to the Bank by its partners are dependent on business profits, there is little incentive for the partners to conceal their problems from the bank, and the danger may indeed be that they may pretend that their results are worse than they really are. The Bank is directly involved in some of the partnerships, particularly when they depend on scarce raw materials or other inputs which can only be accessed on a large scale or through contacts with senior government officials.

The Bank has a total of ten professional staff, of whom seven are women. This includes three field staff, and three other customer service staff in the office, who maintain regular contact with the partners. They keep control accounts for each partnership at the branch, including those businesses whose owners are illiterate and therefore maintain no accounts for themselves, and disbursements of working capital are made only as needed; this ensures that the Bank is kept aware of the current operations, and it also limits the Bank's exposure if things start to go seriously wrong.

A typical short-term trade partnership was between the Bank and a small trader who purchased sesame seed and re-sold it after four months. The arrangement stipulated that the trader would take 25 per cent of the eventual profit for his management; the balance of the profit was to be distributed on the same proportion as the partners' original investment. In the event the bank made a return of 45 per cent on its investment, on an annualised basis, while the trader made 108 per cent, including his management share.

Another typical client of the SIB Omdurman Productive Families branch started her tailoring business in 1991, with an investment of approximately three hundred and fifty dollars. The business prospered, and by 1993 the fixed assets were worth about sixteen hundred dollars. She needed more working capital to finance its expansion, since she was putting out an increasing proportion of the work to local women, and selling to traders who also needed credit.

She therefore entered into a partnership with the SIB under which the bank provided finance up to the same amount as her own capital of $ 1,600; she was allocated 30 per cent of the profit for her management, and the balance was to be shared equally with the bank, on the same basis as their respective investments. Her profits are now averaging about $ 250 per month; her share of this amounts to a return of about 10 per cent a month on her investment, while the Bank is receiving about 5 per cent a month on its money. The high, erratic and undocumented inflation rate means that it is impossible to convert these figures to 'real' returns, but as the nominal profits increase, so does the return to the partners. Under these circumstances, no other form of lending would be viable.

Because of the success of the Omdurman Productive Families branch another branch of the same kind has been opened in Wad Medani, to the South of Khartoum, and the Bank has also decided to open five similar branches in other parts of the capital and elsewhere, because of the success of the initial pilot.

(This case was produced with the assistance of Ms. Nawal Adam, of the Small Business Research Group, Faculty of Economics, University of Gezira, Wad Medani, Sudan.)

Comments and Questions

Islamic approaches to credit have received a great deal of academic attention in recent years, but there has been little reference to their practical application, particularly for smaller enterprises. A recent study found that some attempts had been made to use profit-sharing or Musharaka partnerships in Jordan, Malaysia and Afghanistan, but these had been very limited. Both lenders and their clients seemed to prefer the Murabaha or 'administrative charges' approach, which avoids the letter of religious strictures against fixed interest but is in effect very little different from 'Western' banking practice. The Sudan Islamic Bank seemed to be the only formal institution which was engaged on a significant scale in successful application of Islamic partnership methods for small or microenterprises, anywhere.

The system does have many advantages, however, quite apart from its moral or religious aspects. Inflation is not as widespread or serious as it was, but figures of ten or twenty per cent or more a year are still common. Even ten per cent inflation halves the value of funds in six years, so a system which avoids this must be worth consideration. More critically, perhaps, partnership financing avoids the 'double burden' of loan repayment and loss of livelihood which is necessarily associated with fixed interest lending; this makes poor borrowers even poorer, but it is also bad business for the lender.

The principles of partnership finance are of course being applied in other ways. Institutional venture capital is a major source of finance for new and particularly for growing businesses in the industrialised and in some less-developed countries, but little of this has reached small or micro-enterprises. The previous case study about the Gazaria island branch of BRAC in Bangladesh shows how the same principles are used informally to share the burden of failure when group members' enterprises fail through no fault of their own. 'Passing the hat round' is a common practice among friends who wish to help those who are in need.

Partnership finance appears to have strong ethical, religious and economic advantages; why then has it not been more widely adopted ? The case study provides some answers, and the following questions may suggest ways in which the problems might be overcome.

1) Partnership financing requires more detailed appraisal of the business proposal, since each partnership must be based on an assessment of the likely profits and agreement on the proportion of the earnings which is to be taken by the owner of the business and the financial partner. Are there ways in which this appraisal can be standardised for certain types of business, or can be delegated to others, to minimise the cost to the financial partner ?

2) The business owners must both know how much profit they have made, and be willing to report this honestly to their financial partners. Can the assessment and reporting of profits (or losses) in some way be delegated through the use of groups or other bodies, to ensure honesty and to 'off-load' some part of the financial partner's costs ?

3) Even if the whole system of partnership financing, with or without its religious implications, cannot be applied, are there some aspects of the system which can be used to overcome one or other of the problems of inflation and the 'double burden' of loss ?

CHAPTER 9

THE LAXMI MAHILA SANGAM AND MYRADA, KARNATAKA STATE, INDIA

Early in 1991 13 poor women in Muganahally village, some eighty km from the city of Bangalore in Karnataka State of India, decided to join together and start a 'Sangham', or informal group, under the guidance of Myrada, a large NGO which had been carrying out an integrated rural development project in the area since 1987.

Myrada had been assisting people in many different ways; they ran a variety of training courses in various aspects of farming and small-scale enterprise, they helped with watershed management, forestry and irrigation, with health and education programmes, and in many other ways. All the activities, however, were carried out through groups, since Myrada believed that poor rural people could best be helped if they empowered themselves by working together; the main task of the Myrada extension officers, who each covered about 2,500 people in around six villages, was to help people like the women in Muganahally village in the difficult process of forming a unified group which was strong enough to undertake a variety of development activities.

The 13 women approached their local extension worker and he started to work with them. They agreed that they would hold a weekly meeting every Wednesday evening at 9.30 pm; like most of the 123 groups in the area, they preferred to meet in the evenings because they had to take care of their children, work in the fields or do casual labour in the daylight hours; after dark they were less occupied. At first some of their husbands objected to their wives going out alone at night, and one or two even threatened to beat them if they persisted, but the other members encouraged them and went together to visit their husbands and protest. Because there were already many other women's groups in the area, as well as many men's groups, the men eventually agreed to allow their wives to go out, and they even started to help with the cooking and taking care of children, which they had never done before.

The Myrada worker suggested that the women should appoint two members as their representatives, to coordinate their meetings; they agreed with him not to have a single chairperson or president, and that they would appoint new representatives each year.

After one or two meetings the women agreed that they would each save a minimum of five rupees every week. This was a substantial sum for them, since many of their families lived on less than three thousand rupees a year, and the normal daily wage for casual labour was about ten or fifteen rupees. The Myrada extension worker gave them each a savings passbook, and made the appropriate entries; he also gave them a simple cashbook, and started to teach one of the representatives, who could read and write a few words, how to enter the savings in the books, and how to keep other records.

He also suggested that they should put their accumulated savings in a pass book account at the local branch of the Canara Bank, a large nationalised bank. Earlier groups had opened their accounts in the names of two representative members, since the banks were not allowed to have accounts in the names of informal groups, but this regulation had recently been changed so the Muganahally women were able to have their account in their group name. They decided to call themselves the Laxmi Mahila Sangham, since Laxmi is the goddess of wealth, and Mahila means women; they hoped it would help them to escape from poverty.

The bank paid an interest of only six-and-a-half per cent every year, but this was better than nothing, and the Myrada worker pointed out that the money would be safe in the bank, and that the group would have a better chance of borrowing from the bank in the future if they were already its well-established customers.

After a few weeks the extension worker suggested that the women might start borrowing from their accumulated savings; they were very hesitant at first, since they did not wish to lose their money, and many of them had had bad experiences with moneylenders who would often charge ten per cent or more interest every month or even force them to work long hours without pay on their fields or in their houses because they were in debt. They realised now, however, that they would be borrowing from themselves, and that any interest payments would belong to the group and not to an outsider; after long discussion, they agreed to allow one or two members to take small loans. At first they only lent out a proportion of the weekly savings they had collected at the same meeting when the loan was made, but then they became more confident and started to withdraw and make use of some of the money they had earlier deposited in the bank.

They had long discussions about the interest charge they should impose on themselves. At the beginning, they decided to charge ten rupees per hundred per month, since this was what they were used to paying the moneylenders, and the profit would now belong to the group itself. Some of the first borrowers had difficulty in repaying their loans at this rate, however, so they eventually agreed with the Myrada extension worker that they should reduce the rate to one-and-a-half rupees per hundred, per month; he said that this was the same rate that rich people usually paid to the banks.

Quite a number of the women were sometimes able to save rather more than the five rupees, particularly at harvest time, and their savings, together with the interest payments, mounted up quite quickly. In late 1992 the total reached four thousand rupees; at this point, Myrada added the sum of 34,000 rupees to their savings. This was an interest-free loan, which was agreed to be repaid at some future unspecified date when the group would have accumulated enough money of its own or might be able to use bank finance instead. The women were very happy with this, and they were able very quickly to make good use of the new funds since their experience of having their own source of money had encouraged them to have many good ideas.

Other women had observed the success of the group, and the original thirteen allowed several of their friends to join; by the beginning of 1993 the membership had reached twenty-six, and they decided to keep it at that level. They felt that it would be difficult to maintain the spirit of unity and cooperation which they so enjoyed, and they advised later applicants to set up their own new groups.

The women borrow money for a wide range of purposes; about two-thirds of the loans are for farm requirements like seed and fertiliser, simple tools and equipment, cows and goats and small irrigation projects. Most of the other loans are for daily needs like clothing, medicine or food, or for house repairs, but a few women have also borrowed money for simple non-farm activities such as weaving, incense stick rolling or basket making.

So far, nobody has borrowed money for more than ten months, and the group fixes very strict repayment terms, depending on the nature of the investment. The Myrada worker, who still attends every meeting and helps with the records, sometimes advises them to be more lenient. They, however, argue that if one member is allowed to keep the money for longer than she needs it, she is depriving another of the opportunity of using it.

The regular weekly meeting of the group on 8 February 1993 proceeded on the normal plan. The women met at 9.30 pm as usual, in one member's single room hut; there was scarcely room for all of them to sit on the floor or even to stand, and some stood in the doorway for the whole meeting. They started by calling the roll, and found that twenty-four members were present. Three of the women then sang an opening prayer, and they then paid in their savings, by handing their passbooks to the representative with the money folded inside. Every payment was carefully checked and entered in the member's passbook and the group cashbook. One woman whose child was unwell had asked her neighbour to bring her savings contribution for her, and the husband of the other absent member, who was herself ill, came and handed over her five rupees on her behalf; he did not attend the meeting.

When all the savings had been handed over and recorded, the members who had loan repayments due handed over the necessary amounts. They were given individual receipts and the repayments were also entered in their passbooks and in the group's loan account book. Twenty-four of the members had current loans, while two others had completed repayments of earlier loans and had not yet re-borrowed. Several members had two or even three loans at the same time, of varying maturities, for different purposes, and these were separately recorded in the books.

Shanti was one of the members who made her final repayment at the meeting. She had borrowed Rs. 300 to have a steel tip fitted on her plough, and had repaid the loan in three monthly instalments of Rs. 100 each, plus a total of nine rupees interest. She was confident that the additional yield of millet from her field would be worth at least Rs. 500, because of the deeper cultivation, and she thought the plough would last about ten years with proper maintenance.

The representative collected a total of Rs. 291 from the savings and loan repayments. If it was decided later in the meeting that any loans were to be disbursed, this money would be used for this purpose; any balance would be paid into the group's savings account the next morning. If the cash collected was not enough to cover the loans to be disbursed, the representatives would withdraw the necessary cash from the account the next day and hand it over to the borrowers.

The women considered that any repayment which was not paid on the date it was due was overdue and their records showed that a total of Rs. 820, from seven members, was overdue by that definition. None of the amounts was overdue for more than four weeks, and during the two years of the group's existence nobody had ever failed to repay a loan. On one or two occasions members had asked the group to reschedule their repayments because of sickness or other problems, but they had eventually paid their dues, along with the interest owed. The Myrada worker had showed them how to calculate the interest each month, on the actual balance outstanding, so this did not give them any problems.

After this the representative asked if any members wanted to apply for new loans; this was normally the longest part of the meeting since they discussed every proposal at some length. Since they were all neighbours they were very familiar with one another and knew very well the capacity of each one of them. Nevertheless, they used to discuss each application at some length, to be sure that nobody borrowed more than the abilities and resources of her family would allow, and they also considered the repayment schedule in some detail. The Myrada worker only became involved in these discussions when they asked him, and he usually found that the women were tougher on themselves than he was; he often had to support an application which the members wanted to turn down, or to argue for more lenient repayment schedules.

On this occasion, however, there were no new applications. The representative, with the assistance of the Myrada worker, had filled in all the books as the meeting progressed, so that they were completely up to date. The loan record book showed that their members owed the group a total of Rs. 40,700; the total of the members' savings as recorded in their passbooks had reached Rs. 6766, and the group's own passbook with the Canara Bank showed a credit balance of Rs. 1,077. They had not repaid any of the Myrada loan, and the representative had Rs. 291 cash which she had just collected from the members savings and repayments; as was the normal practice, she proposed to pay this into the bank the next day. The loan record also showed that the group had accumulated a total of Rs. 1,302 in interest payments.

After some brief discussion as to how they might collaborate with other groups in the area in making some improvements to the local school building, the meeting was adjourned shortly after midnight. Some of the members' husbands were waiting outside in the dark to escort their wives home, but most of the women walked home together, discussing their plans for the future.

(The exchange rate is approximately Rs. 35 = $ 1.00)

Comments and Questions

This case study introduces a different sort of group from those which were described in the Grameen Bank and BRAC cases from Bangladesh. Those groups played a critical role in selecting borrowers, appraising the proposals and ensuring recovery, but they did not act as principals in the financial transactions. The members' and the groups' savings were deposited with BRAC, and the members borrowed from BRAC; the groups were facilitating intermediaries.

The Laxmi Mahila Sangam, however, is itself a micro-bank. The members save with it, and borrow from it, it has its own bank account, and it borrows money from Myrada to supplement its members' funds so that it can lend them more than their own savings would allow. It also accumulates whatever surplus it makes on the transactions, as its own capital.

Several of the case studies which follow later describe similar systems, which have evolved in different ways, but Myrada was one of the pioneers of this form of financial intermediation in India. Myrada's own methods have changed substantially since the material for this case study was obtained, and the groups are now borrowing from banks such as Canara Bank rather than from Myrada, but the fundamental principles of the independence of the groups as financial entities in their own right still applies.

It may be useful to consider the following questions:

1) Put together a simple 'balance sheet' for the Laxmi Mahila Sangam, showing where it has obtained its money from and how it is being used. Does it 'balance', and what does it show abut the financial position of the group ? (This is a very simple exercise, but readers who are not familiar with accounts should do it, in order to enhance their understanding of the similar figures which are included in the later case studies.)

2) In what ways does the Laxmi Mahila Sangam differ from the BRAC groups described in the previous case study, in addition to its financial functions ?

3) Does membership of the Laxmi Mahila Sangam demand more or less of the members than the BRAC or Grameen Bank groups, and does it give them more, in terms of 'empowerment' ? Which is preferable, from the members' point of view ?

4) Myrada gave the Laxmi Mahila Sangam a large interest-free loan. Was this wise, should it have been a grant rather than a loan, or should the terms and conditions of the loan have been different ? Should NGOs such as Myrada become involved in lending to groups such as the Laxmi Mahila Sangam, or should they leave that to the banks ?

5) What role does the Myrada field worker play in the management and direction of the Laxmi Mahila Sangam ? Does he do too much, or too little, and for how long is it likely to be necessary for this role to continue ?

6) The Laxmi Mahila Sangam was effectively formed by Myrada. Is it necessary for NGOs or other outsiders to form such groups, or do they already exist, needing only to be identified and possibly trained to act as financial intermediaries ?

CHAPTER 10

PRIDE AND KREP, TWO EXAMPLES FROM MACHAKOS, KENYA

The Local Environment

Machakos is a district headquarters town of some 30,000 people, located about one hour by road from Nairobi, the capital of Kenya. The town serves a large predominantly rural area with a population of around two million. There is little formal industry, except for a medium-sized fruit processing factory in the hills some 10 km away. Apart from the local administration the main economic activity is to serve the surrounding agricultural area. Rainfall is low and erratic, and most of the rural people are semi-subsistence farmers, with small stony holdings growing maize, beans, chick-peas and a small amount of cotton.

Many of the men serve in the Kenyan army or police, outside the area, and others travel daily or weekly to Nairobi for work. In spite of their earnings, however, Machakos is one of the poorer parts of Kenya, and it is frequently necessary for the government to provide relief food to the poorer people of the area.

There is nevertheless a large and active market in the town, where well over a thousand people operate small stalls selling second-hand clothes, vegetables, basic foodstuffs and other necessities. There are also over a hundred small informal workshops, making clothing, furniture, recycled rubber sandals, ploughs and other simple metal items. Apart from a small area of concrete hard-standing, and a small shelter for some carpenters, these businesses operate from shacks or in the open, in unplanned areas without roads, drainage or other facilities.

Barclays Bank, Standard Chartered and the Kenya Commercial Bank, as well as the Kenya Cooperative Bank, all have branches in Machakos, serving the government and its employees, the larger farmers and the few larger Asian and African owned trading firms. Few if any of the people who run the town's informal businesses are able to borrow money from these banks. If they can save the rather high minimum, they can open savings accounts, but they do not have the collateral needed to obtain credit.

PRIDE, A Grameen Bank Bangladesh 'Replication'

Promotion of Rural Initiatives and Development Enterprises, Kenya (PRIDE), was established in 1989, with the objective of providing sustainable financial services to small-scale businesses in the rural towns of Kenya. It was loosely affiliated to PRIDE Africa, which originated from an American NGO, and had operations in Tanzania and Guinea as well as in Kenya. PRIDE's third office was established in February 1992 in Machakos.

By 1994 PRIDE had branches in eleven of the smaller rural towns in Kenya, including Machakos. During its early years, management had come to realise that it was not economic to serve enterprises in scattered rural communities; they decided to focus on existing businesses in towns of around 10,000 people or more, where there was sufficient demand within a five-kilometre radius to justify an office.

The PRIDE system is based on the one pioneered by the Grameen Bank in Bangladesh, with substantial local variations. Prospective borrowers are asked to organise themselves into economic groups (EGs) of five people. They appoint a chairman and a secretary, and ten of these EGS are assembled into a Market Enterprise Committee (MEC) of fifty people. The members of the MEC then attend a small number of training sessions, at which the principles of the PRIDE system are carefully explained to them. Originally, PRIDE had insisted that all prospective members should take a simple business management course, but this was found to be a waste of time since the book-keeping and other skills they were taught were of little practical value to them.

The MEC elects a President, Treasurer and Secretary from the office holders of its constituent EGs, and the EGs meet in their MEC, in the PRIDE office in town, at a specific time on a specific day every week. Each member pays a fee of 100 Kenya shillings, or about US $ 2.00, on joining, and they have to save a further 100 shillings every week, as long as they wish to remain as members.

After the members of an EG have demonstrated their commitment by meeting and saving regularly every week for eight weeks, two of them become eligible for a loan, of a maximum of 10,000 shillings, or about US $ 500, repayable over fifty weeks, at 20 per cent 'flat' rate of interest calculated on the initial principal, which amounts to a real rate of about 38 per cent on the declining balance. After a further four weeks of regular meetings, saving and repayment, two more members can borrow, and four weeks later the last member, usually the chairman, is eligible for a loan.

The members' weekly savings are used to form the loan insurance fund (LIF); each group is liable for its members' repayments, and in case of default the group's LIF can be seized by PRIDE to cover any losses. Because of this obligation, and because nobody in a group can borrow if any one is in arrears, the members ensure that everyone is up to date in repayments; in cases of hardship, they may informally help one another out, and exercise an informal right to seize the fellow member's property in case of wilful default.

After a member has satisfactorily repaid a first loan of 10,000 shillings, he becomes eligible for a second loan of 20,000 shillings, also repayable over 50 weeks. He can then proceed to a third loan of 30,000 shillings, repayable over 65 weeks, and finally a fourth loan of 50,000 shillings, repayable over 100 weeks. Thereafter, it is envisaged that members will be able to 'graduate' to borrowing from a commercial bank, but so far this has not happened.

PRIDE itself is a good customer of one of the large commercial banks in Machakos, whose branch is only a few metres from the PRIDE office, and the PRIDE staff have personally introduced to this bank some of its members who it believes should be ready to 'graduate'. Neither the bank staff nor the members however, are enthusiastic, and those members who are approaching the last loan are trying to persuade PRIDE to allow them to borrow larger sums from itself, rather than handing them over to, what they perceive as, the unwelcoming and bureaucratic banks.

If a member wishes, of course, he can remain within the PRIDE system by taking repeated loans under the ceiling amounts; in Machakos, 1426 loans had been disbursed by November 1994, for a total of 14.5 million shillings, roughly equivalent in purchasing power to $ 300,000. One member had taken five loans, nine had taken four, while there was one member each on the first second and third loan. The on-time repayment rate was 99.5 per cent, excluding the effect of repayments earlier than scheduled, and the branch was approaching the level of 20 MECs, or 1000 members, which PRIDE had found was the optimum for one branch.

By November 1994 there were 910 active members of the Machakos branch, organised into 17 MECs. Just over half the members were women; most of the EGs and MECs included women and men, and although the men's loans were on average slightly larger, and their repayment rate slightly worse, there was little significant difference in the performance of men and women.

Over three-quarters of the loans were for small trading businesses; the balance was made up of loans for service activities such a hairdressing, restaurants and vehicle repair, and manufacturing, such as carpentry, simple metal work, bakeries and tailors.

Jane Luko was a typical member of the PRIDE Machakos office. She had started her knitting business in January 1994, using a second-hand machine which she had bought for 10,000 shillings, on credit from a friend. The machine, along with her stocks, was burned in a fire in May, but she restarted with a rented machine and by November she was making a profit of almost 3,000 shillings a month, after paying herself a monthly wage of 3,600 shillings.

She joined PRIDE in October 1994, with the intention of taking a 10,000 shillings loan to repay her friend, and then to borrow again to expand her business. Her fellow EG members knew her well, and they were confident that she would be able to repay the weekly instalments of 240 shillings on her first loan out of her business' earnings.

The Machakos office of PRIDE was located on the first floor of a modest office building in the town; it had a small room for the manager and his two credit officers, and a telephone, but most of the space was taken by two meeting rooms to cope with the 17 weekly MEC meetings which took place. These meetings, record keeping and accounts and occasional visits to members kept the staff fully occupied. Each room was furnished with ten rows of simple benches, seating five people each, so that the members of each EG could sit together, and it was easy to check on attendance. There was also a small space where members could put property which they had seized from their fellows in cases of default.

The three staff members lived in the town, although they were not natives of Machakos. PRIDE had found that it was necessary to move staff between branches every three years or so, since excessive local familiarity could lead to illegitimate pressures for special favours. Since all the members were within a five-kilometre radius, the staff carried out their routine visits on foot, and the branch had no vehicles of any kind.

PRIDE prides itself on being a 'learning organisation', and many changes have been introduced since its formation, as a result of field experience. After a MEC has been in existence for a year or more, it only has to meet every two weeks, and after a further year the meetings need only take place once a month. At the beginning, PRIDE had insisted that the EGs and the MECs maintain their membership by replacing members who had left the area, closed their businesses or had been expelled for poor repayment. It was later concluded that this was not good for group cohesion, and the MECs and EGs are now permitted to lose members without replacing them.

PRIDE aims to attain sustainability, and perhaps, eventually become an independent financial institution; it is therefore necessary for each branch to work towards covering all its costs. As on 14 November 1994, the financial position of the Machakos branch was approximately as follows (amounts in Kenyan shillings):

Balance Sheet as on 16.11.94

Assets		Liabilities	
Cash	80,000	LIF	3,000,000
Bank	650,000	Bonus owed to members	300,000
Furniture/fittings	100,000	Head office	3,030,000
Advances	5,500,000		
Total	6,330,000		6,330,000

Annual Profit and Loss at the November 1994 operation level

Income		
Interest on loans at 38 per cent		2,090,000
Registration and application fees		75,000
Total income		2,165,000
Expenses		
Bonus 10 per cent on LIF	300,000	
Wages	660,000	
Rent	96,000	
Phone	60,000	
Stationery	50,000	
Bank charges	3,000	
Bad debts	9,000	
Head office	700,000	
(7.7 million shillings divided by 11 offices)		
Total expenses	1,878,000	
Profit		287,000

PRIDE recognised that the LIF was effectively a form of forced savings, and it made up a substantial proportion of the funds available for lending, particularly in a mature branch such as Machakos. PRIDE therefore credited each member's LIF account with an annual 'bonus' of ten per cent. This was much lower than the interest paid on long-term savings accounts by the commercial banks, but the banks demanded minimum opening deposits and balances of 500 shillings or more, and it was competitive with the post office savings bank rate. Members could not withdraw their LIF, or the bonus, unless and until they left PRIDE, since their LIF was a form of guarantee against non-repayment.

In addition to the LIF, PRIDE has obtained its funding from a number of different sources. In its early years, it relied heavily on grants from the United States and other donors, and by November 1994 about 80 per cent of its total capital, apart from the LIF, still came from grants. PRIDE had also obtained concessional loans from two commercial banks and a local foundation, at an average rate of interest of around eight per cent, but the management realised that they could not rely on grants and cheap loans for ever. They were determined to bring the organisation to a level where it could raise money on the commercial market, where funds currently cost about twenty per cent, and the Machakos branch manager, like all his colleagues, was very aware of this goal.

KREP's Self-help Group Lending

The Kenya Rural Enterprises Programme (KREP) was another quite different micro-finance organisation which also operated in Machakos. KREP was started in the mid-1970s as a project of the United States Agency for International Development, as a means of advising and where necessary financing some of the large and growing number of local and foreign non-government organisations (NGO) which were then becoming involved in various aspects of enterprise development.

KREP started by working only with other NGOs; it ran training courses for their staff, it provided advisory services and extended financial assistance, by covering running costs and providing money for revolving loan funds of various kinds. In due course, however, the staff came to feel that they wanted first-hand experience; they were frustrated by the difficulties they had with some of their partners, and they also felt that they could only advise and assist other agencies if they themselves were working in the same field and had some practical experience.

KREP therefore started to offer loans to a small number of group enterprises, such as community-owned maize mills or women's producer groups. Like most other programmes of this sort, this soon ran into difficulties; the group business suffered from a host of management problems, and the KREP staff had to spend a great deal of time with each group; even if they did, the repayment rate of the loans was often under thirty per cent.

In 1989 KREP switched its emphasis to 'minimalist' credit. Some members of its staff visited Bangladesh to study the operations of Grameen Bank and other micro-finance institutions which used similar systems, and they introduced their own adaptation of this group-based lending system to Kenya. It was called the Juhudi system. The field staff helped local micro-business people to form themselves into 'watanus', or groups of five, which in turn met in juhudis of six watanus. KREP lent money to the individual members, through this two-tier group mechanism.

This system worked well; repayments were generally over 95 per cent, and by 1994 KREP had opened several offices throughout the country to offer this form of credit. A number of these were approaching the point where the interest earnings from the loans covered their cost of operations, and some of them were even able to make a small contribution to the cost of head-office administration. Most of the actual capital was provided free of charge, by numerous donors; a small amount was lent by the local banks at subsidised rates of interest.

KREP also continued to assist other NGOs. Several of them started group-based lending on the Grameen Bank model; KREP trained some of their staff, and many of them, such as PRIDE, borrowed money from KREP, again at low rates of interest, to finance their own operations.

KREP was still necessarily involved with a number of group enterprises which had borrowed money and had still not repaid. Frequently, members of these groups asked the KREP field staff whether they, as individuals rather than as a group, could borrow money from PRIDE for their own businesses. They knew very well that their group enterprises were unsuccessful, but they all had their own individual businesses as well, and many of them wanted to borrow money to expand these.

Most of these people, and particularly the women, were already members of their own informal rotating savings and credit groups (ROSCAs), or merry-go-rounds, which were known by various local names. These groups provided a very useful source of money, but the loans were necessarily limited to the total sum that the group could save, and each member had to wait her turn; it was not always possible to borrow money when it was needed.

In June 1991 the KREP staff in Meru, a small town on the slopes of Mt. Kenya, were approached by two such groups whose members wanted to borrow money; they asked the groups to form themselves into the watanu and juhudi structure, but the women protested that they already had strong and long-standing groups of their own; why should they not be allowed to borrow money right away?

The KREP staff realised that these ROSCAs might be a ready-made channel whereby KREP could extend financial assistance to larger numbers of rural women. They obtained permission from KREP head office to extend small loans to the two groups, on an experimental basis, to enable them in their turn to lend more money to their members.

The experiment was an immediate success. The groups repaid their loans exactly as scheduled, and it seemed to be far quicker, and easier, to lend money to existing groups of this sort than to go through the long process of developing watanus and juhudis which required the KREP staff and prospective borrowers to spend a great deal of time on meetings and so on, before any loans could be offered at all.

This method of lending soon came to be known as the 'chikola' system, using a word by which RCSCAs were known to the Giriama tribe on the coast of Kenya. The KREP management decided to extend it to other areas, and by November 1994 it was being offered through 14 offices including Machakos; a total of 150 groups, with 3,750 members, were borrowing over 75 million shillings from KREP. The on-time repayment rate, expressed as the per centage of payments which were made on the due day compared with the payments which were due on that day, including any accumulated arrears, was 97.4 per cent, and the whole operation seemed to be simpler and more economical for KREP and for its customers.

The Tumaini, or 'Hope' group in Machakos started in 1991. The 26 members, all women, were all involved in business activities of some sort. They originally came together because the salaried people in the town, such as school teachers and civil servants, used to look down on business women. The members of the Tumaini group felt the need for a social group of their own. They wanted to assert their independence, and also to avoid unnecessary competition between one another in the market.

They had started a merry-go-round not only as a source of capital but also as a form of self-help association. They raised funds when members were ill or needed money for funerals or other occasions, and they met informally to discuss and share their business problems. They found that their regular monthly contributions of 100 shillings, and the allocation of the resulting 'pot' to one member, provided a routine around which their other activities could grow.

KREP started work in Machakos in early 1992. After an initial six months of enquiries through local government staff, avoiding any political groupings but ensuring that the local officials were fully informed about what it was doing, it had identified ten groups with the potential to be viable customers for Chikola loans. This was felt to be the minimum for a viable office.

The Tumaini group had heard about KREP, but at first they were reluctant to make an approach because they thought this would expose them to taxation, or political influences. After some time they heard that other similar groups had benefited from association with KREP, and they approached the local office, which was a single room on the second floor in a small office building on the edge of the town.

The KREP Machakos manager, who ran the office on his own with one messenger, asked them about their activities. He satisfied himself that they had been operating their rotating savings and credit operation for over a year, and he explained the way in which the KREP chikola system operated. The representatives of the Tumaini group agreed that they would like to go further, and the KREP manager then made an appointment to meet the group at one of its regular monthly savings meetings. He observed the way they conducted the meeting, he inspected their attendance and savings records, and then explained the procedure to the whole group.

They would have to register themselves with the local office of the Ministry of Local Government and Social Services, since Kenyan law required that any formal groups should be registered. The law only allowed groups of between twenty and thirty members to register at this level, and KREP had found that this number was also suitable for chikola lending. Registration would also enable them to open a bank account in the group's name at the Machakos bank through which KREP conducted its lending. They already had an account in the names of their president and secretary, but KREP required that it should be in the name of the group itself.

He also explained that they would have to discuss among themselves how much each one of them wanted to borrow, up to a maximum of 30,000 shillings per member, for one year. They would then have to save ten per cent of the total sum they wanted and deposit this in their new savings account.

It was understood that the group could not touch this money until the loan was totally repaid. This was not legally mandated to KREP, since KREP did not want to imply in any way that they did not trust the groups, and they wanted the groups to regard this money as a fund which would eventually enable them to run their own credit scheme without borrowing from KREP. The group would then have to prepare a written application for the loan, and submit it to the manager, along with their registration certificate and savings bank passbook, and an application fee of one per cent of the amount they wanted to borrow.

The KREP manager also visited each of the members at her place of business. He wanted to be sure that they all were in business, since KREP charged interest of about three per cent a month on loans it made to such groups; the members would not be able to repay if their loans were not invested in profitable businesses.

Although there were a few objective criteria for accepting a group, such as the minimum period of a year's savings and registration, the manager's assessment was mainly subjective. He only accepted about one in three of the groups who approached him, and some offices rejected nine out of ten. They knew that there were large numbers of groups who wanted funds, and that the success of the Chikola programme depended on their ability to screen and eliminate the weaker groups, or those which had come together just to get KREP loans; as the programme became better known, this type of 'phony' group became more common.

The members then consulted among themselves, and decided that they wanted to proceed. They met in their small informal neighbourhood groups of five or six members, and discussed the ways in which this new money would help them to expand their businesses. One woman said that she would be able to buy 150 kg. of sugar at a time for her shop instead of 50 kg.; this would be slightly cheaper, but it would also save travelling time and would reduce the danger of running out of stock.

Another woman decided to buy some new equipment and materials for her hairdressing business. A third member realised that a loan of the scale that KREP offered would mean that she could restock her general shop once a week instead of every day, and another who employed two girls sewing ready-made garments decided to buy a new machine, since she knew a competent seamstress who was looking for a job and she was confident she could sell the extra production. Since they knew each other very well, they were able to discuss their ideas openly; as they said, "we know what each of us can manage."

Three of the members who had jobs and were planning to start businesses in due course did not want to borrow at this stage. The individual requirements of the remaining 23 members ranged from 15,000 to 25,000 shillings, and they calculated that they would need a total of 485,000 shillings. This was well below the maximum allowed, and each member then contributed ten per cent of the loan she wanted; the total sum of 48,500 shillings was deposited in their new bank account. They also put together a further one per cent of the total, for the application fee, and submitted their complete application to the Machakos office of KREP.

He read through it carefully, ensuring that the individual members' loans were consistent with what he had seen of their businesses, and he then sent it to the KREP head office in Nairobi, by courier. It was quite rare for the head office to turn down an application which had been approved in the field, and he knew that a decision would be made, and communicated to him, within ten working days, or a maximum of two weeks.

Approval for the Tumaini group came in six days; the head office sent him a legal agreement between KREP and the Tumaini group, already signed by the managing director of KREP. The Machakos manager took this to a especially convened meeting of the group. He carefully explained all the terms; the loan was to be repaid over twelve months, starting on the last day of the month in which the loan would be disbursed, or 30 November 1993; the group would not be allowed to repay ahead of schedule, and if any repayments were late KREP would have the right to collect overdues from the group's savings account.

The members all agreed; they then each had to sign the loan agreement, and to give their identity card number. The Machakos manager sent the signed agreement back to head office; three days later he went to the bank to ensure that the money had been sent by telegraphic transfer from Nairobi. The Tumaini women convened another meeting; the KREP manager handed over a cheque in favour of the group, drawn on the KREP account at the Machakos branch.

The Treasurer of the group then wrote out a cheque to each member for whatever sum had been agreed. The KREP manager also ensured that the treasurer filled out a standing order from the group's account to the KREP account, for the monthly instalment of 48,500 shillings; this was calculated by adding 20 per cent to the total amount of the loan, and dividing the result into twelve monthly payments. He had already explained to the group that this worked out to a real rate of interest of about 36 per cent, on the declining balance.

The Tumaini group was free to charge its members whatever rate of interest it wanted for their loans, since the loan agreement was between KREP and the group, and the group's loans to its members were under its control. The Tumaini group had already decided to calculate the interest at a rate of three per cent per month, on declining balance; this amounted to about one per cent more than the interest that the group had to pay to KREP. Some groups, such as one in Nyeri, a town in Central Kenya, had fixed an interest rate of five per cent a month; the decision was theirs.

The manager impressed on the members that they should be sure to make their monthly repayments to the group, and to bank the total sum, at the latest by the end of each month. The standing order was for the fifth day of each month, and if the money was not in the bank in time, KREP would not be paid but in addition the group would have to pay a heavy penalty fee to the bank.

KREP had no form of guarantee or security from the group, apart from its agreed right to draw repayments from their ten per cent deposit if necessary, but the Tumaini women had designed a very strict system to control their own repayments to their group. Each member signed a legal agreement with the group, which they had asked a lawyer to prepare, and she also had to agree to hand over property to a value of at least 110 per cent of her loan in the event of default. This might include a sewing machine or hair-dryer from her business, or personal property such as home furniture or a radio. They also agreed that any member who repaid late would have to pay a fine of 500 shillings to the group. Some other groups demanded that members obtain written guarantees from friends who could cover their obligations if necessary, and the Tumaini women had heard of cases when these guarantees had to be enforced.

At the beginning of November 1994 each of the Tumaini women had repaid her loan to the group, and the whole loan from KREP had been cleared exactly as agreed. The group members had continued their own regular savings as before, although KREP did not demand this; they had each put 100 shillings into the kitty each month, plus 50 shillings to pay for tea and refreshments and whatever repayment they owed on their loan. They had not given the kitty to a member as before, however, since they already had their loans from the KREP money, and as a result the Tumaini women had accumulated 52,000 shillings in a deposit account which earned them 24 per cent interest; they also had their savings account with the 48,500 shillings which they had to contribute as a condition of obtaining the KREP loan.

The members now had to decide whether they wanted to take a new loan from KREP; they could borrow up to 60,000 shillings each this time, and repay over two years if they wished, and they could then take a third loan for up to 120,000 shillings each, also repayable over two years, and a fourth loan for up to 200,000 shillings each, again for a maximum of two years. They were sure that they would borrow again, since nearly all of their businesses had benefited from the first loans, even though economic conditions had been poor. KREP however, insisted on a gap of at least a month between the repayment of one loan and disbursing another, so the women had at least three weeks in which to decide.

Some of the members of the Tumaini group wanted to learn more about management before trying to expand their businesses further. They asked whether KREP could provide some training for them, but the manager said that it was not possible; all he could do was to refer them to one or other of the numerous small business management training institutions, some of which operated in Machakos.

The Kieni Kia Sokoni, or "Light of the Market" group was another customer of the KREP Machakos branch. They started in 1992 with twenty men and six women members, but one man had lost interest and two women had to be expelled because they did not attend meetings or make their repayments on time. The group had pressed them and finally persuaded them to pay, but had then expelled them in order to avoid further trouble.

The 23 remaining members had taken a loan of 350,000 shillings in August 1993; this had been repaid on time, and they then took a second loan of 1,100,000 shillings in September 1994; although they could have repaid this over two years, they agreed to repay it in one year because they had not had any difficulty in repaying the first loan. In addition, they wanted to save interest payments, and to have the option to progress to bigger loans if they wanted.

At the beginning of November 1994 the Kieni Kia Sokoni group had 114,225 shillings in a fixed deposit account, as well as 12,566 shillings in a savings account. They had accumulated this money from their routine weekly merry-go-round contributions of 50 shillings, which, like the Tumaini group they had continued to make, but not to withdraw, after receiving the KREP loan. They also had 110,000 shillings in a savings account as a ten per cent deposit against their loan from KREP; they had accumulated this money from one-off contributions from members according to the amounts each wanted to borrow.

Some members of the group thought that they should run their credit fund from their own resources after repaying the second loan, since they had already accumulated a substantial sum, and they did not want to go on paying interest to KREP. Others wanted right away to borrow far larger sums than were allowed by KREP, even for the fourth and subsequent loans.

The KREP manager suggested that these members should apply to one of the three national commercial banks with branches on Machakos, and he offered to write a reference for them confirming their good record as members of the Kieni Kia Sokoni group which had borrowed from KREP; they laughed at him, and said that although the banks charged only about 25 per cent per year, it took months to get a loan, and it was probably impossible unless you had a land title deed, which most of them did not, and the bank managers also preferred people who had been good customers for many years and whom they knew personally. They wanted KREP to lend them money individually, not through the group, but the manager knew that this was not presently allowed by KREP.

On 30 October 1994 the Machakos office was dealing with 26 groups, with an average of 25 members each. Over half the members were women, and there were all male, all female and mixed groups like the Kieni Kia Sokoni. The manager thought that it should be possible for him to deal with possibly twice as many groups, without additional staff. The financial position of the office was approximately as follows (figures in Kenya shillings):

Assets		Liabilities	
Cash	2,000	Head office loan	12,022,000
Furniture	20,000		
Advances	12,000,000		
Total	12,022,000	Total	12,022,000

Annual Profit and Loss at the October 1994 Operation Level

Income		
Interest on loans at 35 per cent		4,200,000
Application fees		120,000
Total income		4,320,000
Expenses		
Transport	18,000	
Wages	240,000	
Rent	48,000	
Phone	24,000	
Stationery	12,000	
Bank charges	3,000	
Bad debt provision at 5per cent	300,000	
Area office	200,000	
Head office allocation	100,000	
Cost of funds at 20 per cent	2,400,000	
Total expenses	3,345,000	
Profit		975,000

The actual cost of funds to KREP was of course lower than 20 per cent, because most of their money had come in the form of grants and some subsidised loans at 10 per cent interest or less. KREP however, felt that they should impose a more realistic cost on themselves. KREP aimed to become a commercial bank itself in the near future, and the management chose the rate of 20 per cent because this was the approximate rate of interest charged by the banks to large commercial borrowers, and was thus the 'opportunity cost' of funds to a profit-seeking financial institution. This rate was predicted to come down, but it had been over 50 per cent a few months before, and inflation was also running at about 25 per cent per year, having fallen from over 75 per cent a year earlier.

(Note: This case study was written with the help of Mike Oneko, Grace Oloo and Ole Sambu of PRIDE and Aleke Dondo, Nancy Wanjiku Thuo and Rose Mwaniki of KREP.)

(The exchange rate is approximately 50 Kenya Shillings = US $ 1.00.)

Comments and Questions

These two institutions, serving very similar customers in the same quite small rural town, provide an unusual opportunity to compare two different forms of group intermediation. The PRIDE method is, like the BRAC Gazaria case, a 'replication' of the Grameen bank Bangladesh approach, with substantial local modifications. KREP is using a method which is not dissimilar to the Myrada system described in the previous case, although here too there are very important differences.

The case study describes the very different origins of the KREP 'Chikola' method; it was not based on experience elsewhere, but it evolved almost by accident, as a result of pressure from customers who were dissatisfied with the previous system. This is perhaps the ideal source of any new approach, so long as the institution and its staff have the freedom and flexibility to recognise good ideas.

The micro-finance industry includes a wide range of different methods and forms of intermediation, including group-based and individual approaches. Within the group-based systems, however, the two approaches which are described in this case study can be said to represent the two main 'schools'. There is a great deal of debate as to which is 'better'. This case study, and other examples in this book, should demonstrate that both have their advantages and weaknesses, and that each situation requires its own system, based on local conditions, the nature of the institution and, above all, the needs of the proposed clients.

The different methods of operation have important implications for the clients and for the financial institution; the following questions suggest some of the more significant differences:

1) Both PRIDE and KREP are serving small-scale business people, who were not previously able to access formal credit, and the majority of their clients are women. Which of the two systems, if any, appears likely to reach the poorer people, and which is more likely to be better suited for those who are better-off ?

2) Micro-finance is said to 'empower' its clients as well as to improve their incomes. Which of the two systems is the most 'empowering', particularly for women ?

3) The Machakos offices of both PRIDE and KREP are profitable according to the figures. Which of the two systems is the most efficient, in terms of its costs per shilling lent, and which is most likely to be able to survive and grow without any further access to grants or subsidised loans ?

4) The owners of small businesses need financial services which are inexpensive, accessible and flexible; which of the two systems is best, on each count ?

5) Neither of the two institutions was permitted at the time described in the case study to raise savings deposits from the public. The PRIDE

A stall in the Merced Market, Mexico City (Chapter 16)

A Meeting of a Myrads savings and credit group, Kolar District, India (Chapter 9)

Clients of Pride, Machakos, Kenya (Chapter 10)

A 'Chikola' group meeting in Machakos, Kenya (Chapter 10)

Mrs. Nozibeli Ntuli of Mfuleni, South Africa (Chapter 17)

Annual meeting of VVK Madurai (Chapter 18)

A Basix client repaying a crop loan. Near Raichur, India (Chapter 19)

A client of Basix Finance with his new irrigation pump. Near Raichur, India (Chapter 19)

LIF fund was similar to a savings scheme, but in the future both would need to access savings as a source of funds to lend. Which of the two institutions would be more likely to be able to do this successfully ?

6) Both KREP and PRIDE tried to assist their clients to 'graduate' to commercial banks when they seemed to be ready to take larger loans, independent of any group intermediation. Both failed. Should they instead encourage their more successful clients to remain with them by developing new services for them, and possibly cross-subsidise the smaller clients with profits from serving the larger ones, or should they concentrate on their original target market ?

7) The commercial banks appear to be wilfully neglecting an opportunity to take on new customers who have proved their credit-worthiness with PRIDE and KREP. Why are the banks not enthusiastic, can they in some way be encouraged or even compelled to take on these clients, or must the expansion of micro-finance depend solely on the growth of new institutions, such as PRIDE and KREP ?

CHAPTER 11

THE KENYA INDUSTRIAL ESTATES INFORMAL SECTOR PROGRAMME MURANG'A BRANCH

Kenya Industrial Estates (KIE) was established by the Government of Kenya in the late 1960s in an attempt to assist local people to establish manufacturing businesses. It started by constructing an industrial estate in Nairobi, and in the 1970s it built a number of Rural Industrial Development Centres, which were smaller estates in towns around the country, in an effort to encourage regional industrialisation.

KIE soon realised that its clients needed more than premises, and in spite of its name the organisation soon became involved in training, financial services, common facilities and a whole range of other activities. KIE received assistance from numerous donors; their differing agendas, and the influence of local political interests, meant that KIE soon 'lost its way'. Loans were not repaid, in spite or perhaps because of the low interest rates, the subsidised rents for sheds on the estates sometimes went unpaid for years, and like many other small industry-promotion institutions in Africa and elsewhere, by the late 1980s KIE was in serious difficulties.

In 1982 a foreign donor assisted KIE to start a loan programme for smaller informal businesses, but it was mismanaged in the same way as the larger loans, and the rate of repayment was very low. In 1988 GTZ, the German technical assistance organisation, which had been one of the many donors working with KIE, took over this programme with the intention of restructuring it in order to bring KIE back to its original goal of helping local business people to sustain and expand independent businesses.

The design of the programme was to an extent informed by the 'minimalist' approach which was coming into vogue at that time. A comprehensive needs assessment at the beginning of the programme had shown that business people above all, needed access to credit, at a place and time and in amounts which were appropriate for their needs, and at a price which they could afford. Other services might also be needed by some people, but these were secondary to credit.

The restructured programme was called the Informal Sector Loans Programme (ISP); it was directed not at the smallest or at start up enterprises, whose financial needs were already beginning to be served by a number of different organisations, but at existing businesses which had already attained some element of stability, and whose owners had the ambition to grow.

After some initial experiments the programme managers designed a multi-stage system of client recruitment and appraisal, which was by late 1994 being implemented by 25 branches in small towns throughout the country. Three of these branches were more or less moribund, because of mistakes made in the earlier version of the programme, and the ISP management planned to close these down and write off their overdues.

The remaining 21 offices (two other offices had been merged) were actively involved. Some branches were based in existing KIE offices, and others were independent; each branch was staffed by between one and four people, and they were solely responsible for implementing the ISP in their area.

By March 1995 the ISP had lent about 155 million Kenyan shillings to some 3,900 micro and small businesses. Some 4,700 entrepreneurs had been trained in ISP's management orientation programme. At the same time the programme's portfolio showed a portfolio of about one hundred million shillings (about two million dollars) outstanding to some 2,000 business people.

Almost a third of the borrowers were women. This proportion was increasing, both because the ISP wished to help women to overcome the constraints which prevented them from accessing loans by providing equal access to credit for good business people, and also because women's repayment record was generally found to be better than men's. Many of the women clients were tailors, or had hair saloons, but others were running similar enterprises to the men, including carpentry and vehicle repair.

The minimum loan size was 10,000 shillings (about $ 200) and the maximum was 250,000 shillings (about $ 5,000); this overlapped some of the other programmes at the lower end, but the average loan of 50,000 shillings was well above the average of the other micro-enterprise credit programmes. The KIE's formal sector loan programme offered loans from 100,000 shillings to 5,000,000 shillings and had recently been redesigned on a similar basis to the ISP. Many of its surplus staff had been laid off, but this programme did not overlap with the ISP to a significant extent. The ISP loans were still well below level at which commercial bank loans were a reasonable possibility. New clients were not allowed to borrow more than 100,000 shillings unless they had good references from other lenders, but higher sums were available after earlier loans had been satisfactorily repaid.

The ISP adhered strictly to its client eligibility criteria; to be eligible, a business had to have been in existence for at least a year, it normally had between one and twenty employees, its owner must also be its full time manager and it had to have a licence, which could easily be obtained. The programme managers preferred to recruit manufacturing enterprises, but in branches where there were insufficient manufacturers to make up an economic local 'cluster' of around ten clients within a three-kilometre radius, service and trading businesses were also accepted. Staff were not permitted to recruit further than fifty km from their offices, since this was also felt to be uneconomic, and it was intended that the ISP should work towards sustainability.

The ISP was promoted through meetings, seminars, posters and door-to-door canvassing by its staff. Interested and eligible business were required to purchase for 200 shillings a simple opening and closing stock and sales and raw material recording form, which they had to maintain for one month.

After a month, the ISP staff member would visit each prospective client who had bought a form; he would check the eligibility, and would compare the sales and raw material costs from the form with approximate industry standards for value-added per centages which the ISP had prepared. If the raw materials used by a carpentry business, for instance, appeared to be well under 40 per cent or over 60 per cent of sales, the ISP would examine more closely to see if the figures had been properly collected, or if there was some special feature of the business to justify the figures.

The ISP tried to sell a minimum of fifteen forms in the cluster area, in the expectation of approving about ten clients for the next stage of the procedure. This involved an eight-day orientation and training programme, spread over four weeks, for which the applicant had to pay a fee of 500 shillings which covered about a fifth of its total cost. The main purpose of this programme was to assist the applicant to prepare a simple business plan, demonstrating to his own and to the ISP satisfaction that his business was viable and that he had a clear and potentially profitable plan for using whatever sum he was proposing to borrow. At this point a number of clients withdrew, since they had come to realise as a result of the programme that either their plans were not viable or that they could mobilise the necessary funds from within their own businesses, without recourse to a loan.

At this stage a formal loan application was prepared. Proposed purchases of equipment or other items had to be substantiated by a proforma invoice from the supplier, or an informal written agreement to supply if it involved second hand equipment or other informal vendors. The application also had to include the signatures of two guarantors for the loan, who had to be people whose income from whatever source appeared sufficient to cover the applicant's repayments should he himself be unable to pay. In addition, the applicant was required to agree to pledge whatever security he could muster. This was not usually in the form of land title deeds, since few applicants had these, but the ISP would accept as security the existing or proposed new assets of the business, or, as a last resort, the log book of any vehicle the applicant might own. In general, collateral was assessed on its realisable value and also on its value to the client.

Completed loan applications were then approved in a local committee at the branch level, and passed to head office in Nairobi for final approval. Very few applications were turned down at this stage, and the total delay from the end of the training and orientation programme until disbursement of the loan was usually less than a month.

Interest was charged at a rate of 32 per cent, calculated on the reducing balance; this was well above the rate charged by the commercial banks, but below the rates charged by micro-credit programmes such as the Kenya Rural Enterprise Programme (KREP) which were aimed at the smallest enterprises.

Repayment periods were between six months and three years, with one month grace period. Loans could be repaid by standing order, (despite the inefficiency of the banks), by cheque or cash payments at a commercial bank or by cash or cheque to the ISP officer, although this latter method was discouraged except in cases of arrears, because of the security problem.

Clients had to submit a monthly return to the ISP, following the same format as their original sales and raw material purchases form, and the ISP branch officer also made periodic visits to check and advise on progress where necessary, and to collect repayments, particularly in cases of arrears. Every case was also discussed in detail at a quarterly review meeting in each branch office. At the satisfactory completion of repayments, clients were given a certificate of completion and a reference which it was hoped would increase their chances of obtaining credit from a commercial bank. By late 1994 a certain number of clients had 'graduated' to the banks or to the KIE formal sector programme, whose requirements were now very similar to those of the banks.

The ISP exercised its rights to seize collateral or call guarantees on any loan whose repayments were three months or more in arrears, and legal proceedings would be started if the loan was more than six months overdue. By March 1995 the repayment performance was over 93 per cent for the newer loans, calculated as the per centage of repayments made of the total amounts due, including overdues, and the total amount of arrears stood at 19 per cent of the total outstanding portfolio. This average included far worse performances by the three less successful branches, so that the other branches were actually achieving far higher figures.

The ISP was still a department of the KIE, although internal figures were produced to show the performance of each branch and of the programme as a whole. The smallest branch, in Malindi on the coast of Kenya, had about 60 clients, and a total portfolio of some two million shillings, and the largest, in Murang'a, North of Nairobi, served 210 clients, with a portfolio of about eleven million shillings.

The Germans still provided the loan fund on a no interest basis, but they were supporting the project's plan to separate the ISP from KIE and to constitute it as an independent organisation, with the eventual objective of becoming a self-sustaining financial institution, covering its costs and able to generate additional funds on a commercial basis. The ISP was already more than covering its own operating costs in the fiscal half-year results for July to December 1994 for the first time. It was, however, estimated that a significant further expansion of its business and thus access to new sources of funds was needed in order to be able to cover the market cost of its funds by about September 1996. As a result, diversification away from KIE became even more important.

The ISP motto is "go the extra mile", but branch staff are concerned at the effect on their clients of the numerous foreign funded NGO and church credit programmes which offer similar funds but at very low rates of interest and with little pressure for repayment. In 1992/3 the Government had also set up a rural development industry fund of 400 million shillings (eight million dollars), which was lent at six per cent interest, on a mainly political basis before national elections, and of which only a small proportion was expected to be repaid. Clients were not unreasonably reluctant to repay their loans to ISP when they observed what borrowers from other programmes had enjoyed.

When the KIE/ISP was started, its management did its best to distance it from KIE, because of the past record of poor repayments; they wanted clients to realise that the new programme was run on businesslike lines, and that its loans had to be repaid. The head office of the KIE/ISP was shifted out of the main headquarters block in the industrial area of Nairobi, into a small separate building on the same plot. It was more difficult to demonstrate the separation in the field offices, since they were much smaller, but the KIE/ISP employed different staff, and they tried to maintain their separateness in every way.

The Murang'a branch of the KIE had been established when KIE itself was first started, in the early 1970s, and it had offered all the various KIE programmes, including the original unsuccessful informal business loan programme. Some of the same clients who had kept to the terms of their loans had been carried over to the new programme, but the staff successfully showed that it was very different, and they soon established a reputation for efficient, fast and impartial service.

Jane Mukundi was a typical client of the ISP programme of the Murang'a branch. She dropped out of secondary school after two terms in 1975, because her parents had no money. After spending several years at home without work, she was lucky enough in 1981 to join an ILO-sponsored training course in knitting which was run at a 'rehabilitation centre' for unemployed people in the area. In 1983, at the end of this two year course, she received a knitting machine and 500 shillings worth of materials, on a grant basis, and in June 1984 she started her own business.

In 1986 she was introduced to the KIE programme by a friend, and took a loan for 5,000 shillings from the original informal business programme. She repaid this loan on time, unlike many of the clients at this time, and in 1990 she borrowed a further 15,000 shillings to buy raw materials. This enabled her to expand her business substantially; she bought a new knitting machine, hired another one and employed one skilled employee and two apprentices.

This loan was also repaid on time, and in 1993 Jane Mukundi took a third loan of 34,000 shillings for more raw materials. Her business continued to expand; she accumulated enough cash to buy the knitting machine which she had rented, and in 1994 she was preparing to take a fourth loan to finance further growth. She had one employee and three apprentices at that time, and was planning to buy a plot and expand her business still further. She is unmarried, and has one child, but is optimistic for the future.

Francis Kimani was employed as a driver for the Tea Authority, and he then took a job as manager in a saw-mill. He took a number of courses on management and the technical aspects of saw-mills at the local Forest Industrial Training Centre, and then decided to start his own carpentry business with the 50,000 shillings which he had saved from his wages. He set up his business on a plot which he rented for the purpose from the owner of a saw-mill. This meant that he had no problem in getting raw materials.

Some time later, when Francis' business was well established, the owner of this mill decided to sell out, including the land occupied by Francis' carpentry business. The price of the whole concern, including the land, was half a million shillings, but Francis' father, who also owned a saw-mill, was a good customer of a branch of Bank of Baroda. This helped Francis to take a loan from them, and he was thus able to buy the whole plot and the saw-mill.

In 1994, when he had almost repaid the loan from the Bank of Baroda, Francis joined the KIE/ISP programme. He took a loan for 250,000 shillings of which he spent ninety thousand on a new power saw. The balance was used to increase the stock of logs, and to refurbish and improve the saw-mill premises.

A few months later, Francis borrowed a further one million shillings from a local branch of the Bank of Baroda, to buy a lorry for transporting logs from the forest to his saw-mill. He also proposes to approach KIE/

ISP for a further loan, as soon as he has repaid the first one, to buy a second-hand tractor for the logging operations. He realised that the maximum loan is 250,000 shillings and this may not be enough for a suitable tractor, but he hopes to be able to raise the balance from the business.

Francis is very optimistic about the prospects for his business. He now employs six people, including his wife, and there seems to be an insatiable demand for timber in towns near to the coast, such as Voi and Monbasa. He also plans to invest in a high class hotel and other property.

The branch operations of the KIE/ISP did not have separate accounts like the branches of a bank or a financial NGO like KREP or PRIDE, nor did they have their own office equipment and so on since they were usually located in the KIE branch offices, which also housed the management of the regional industrial estates and the other loan programmes. Management did however provide field staff with figures for the performance of their branches. No allowance was made for the cost of funds, since all the money came at no cost from donor sources.

The Murang'a branch was typical of the well-established branches, and its financial position and operating performance at the end of 1994 were approximately as follows:

Approximate Balance Sheet for 31 December 1994

Assets		Liabilities	
Advances	7,728,000	Head office loan	7,728,000

Profit and Loss Account for July to December 1994

Income		
Interest on Loans		996,000
Income from fees etc.		269,000
Total income		1,265,000
Expenses		
Wages	268,000	
Rent	30,000	
Bad debt	6,000	
Administration and other expenses	112,000	
Total expenses	416,000	
Profit		849,000

The Machakos branch of the KIE/ISP was established much later than the one at Murang'a, and it only had about one-third of the loan portfolio. The average loan size was smaller, since more of the clients were new and had thus not reached the stage of taking higher loans. This affected the performance of the office. Management expected the Machakos office to come up to the level of Murang'a in a few years, but even in 1994 the results were not unsatisfactory.

The summarised financial information for the Machakos branch at 31 December 1994 was as follows:

Assets		Liabilities	
Advances	2,669,000	Head office loan	2,669,000

Profit and Loss Account for July to December 1994

Income
Interest on Loans	371,000
Income from fees	82,000
Total income	453,000

Expenses
Wages	182,000	
Rent	30,000	
Bad debt	102,000	
Administration	29,000	
Depreciation and other expenses	20,000	
Total expenses	363,000	
Profit		90,000

(This case study was prepared with the help of Mr. E. Nyaanga and Mr. Gathage, of Kenya Industrial Estates)

(The exchange rate is approximately 50 Kenya Shillings = US $ 1.00.)

Comments and Issues

The business owned by the clients of the KIE/ISP programme are small, or even medium, rather than micro, and it might be argued that it does not belong in a book about micro-finance at all. Most clients start with loans of about $ 150, however, which is well within the range of the other institutions, and the programme does illustrate many of the issues involved in client 'graduation'.

It can indeed be suggested that micro-finance programmes which do not allow their clients to borrow more than one or two hundred dollars are effectively preventing their businesses from progressing to a level where they can offer jobs to the vast majority of peoples who do not want to be self-employed, but to be employed. Micro-credit enables micro-enterprises to earn micro-livings for their owners; surely this is only a stop-gap solution to poverty and unemployment, and the goal should be job-creation, by businesses such as those owned by the clients of the KIE/ISP ?

There are many examples of micro-finance programmes which are similar to those described in the earlier case studies, but there are very few programmes like the KIE/ISP. This may be because it is more difficult to design an effective programme for growing businesses than it is to assist the relatively stagnant businesses of the poor. It is also possible that the commercial banks may be satisfying this market in most places, so that there is no need for new programmes or institutions, although this appears unlikely. For whatever reason, however, finance for growth seems to be less available than finance for survival, and this example shows how growing businesses can be assisted with an integrated programme of finance and training which also appears to cover its costs.

It is interesting to compare the figures for the Machakos branch of this programme with those for the two group-based micro-finance institutions described in the previous case. The Machakos offices of both KREP and PRIDE were running more or less at capacity at the time described, while the KIE/ISP office was at about one-third of its projected level of operation. All are charging interest rates well over the banks, and KIE's interest rate is substantially lower than the other programmes, and it still appears to be perhaps the most profitable of the three. Existing micro-finance institutions which are considering 'trading up', commercial banks whose most profitable customers have usually joined them when they were at the growth stage like Francis Kimani, or newcomers looking for profitable opportunities, can all learn from this experience.

The case raises many important issues, including the following:

1) Should micro-finance institutions concentrate on micro-loans to micro-businesses, or should they aim to 'trade up' with those of their customers whose businesses grow away from the micro-level ?

2) KIE has combined training with lending, in a way which also obtains the information necessary for the lending decision. Can this approach be more widely applied, for smaller, less ambitious businesses, with less-educated owners, in order to improve loan appraisal and make it less expensive ?

3) Should the KIE/ISP increase the maximum amount it is willing to lend, in order to retain customers whose needs go beyond the present limit, should they be passed on to other programmes within KIE, or should they be encouraged to go to commercial banks ?

4) One of the reasons for the entry of so many new institutions into micro-finance, such as NGOs, is that existing institutions have been so damaged by badly designed and badly implemented programmes, that they have lost credibility with their own staff, their potential clients and their sources of finance. KIE was typical of this situation, but the KIE/ISP has overcome the problems. How have they done this, and what can other 'older' institutions learn from their success ?

5) Are the Murang'a and the Machakos branches of the KIE/ISP really profitable ? What costs have been omitted, and what sort of information about their performance should be provided to branch management and staff of such institutions ?

CHAPTER 12

CUTTACK URBAN COOPERATIVE BANK—COLLEGE SQUARE BRANCH DAILY COLLECTION SYSTEM

Cuttack, which used to be the capital of the State of Orissa in eastern India, is a city of about half a million people. Orissa is one of the poorest states of India, and since the capital of the state was moved to the nearby city of Bhubaneswar soon after independence, there has been little development in Cuttack. The central law courts of the state and several of the main educational institutions remained in the city, but apart from this and some traditional silver filigree work and handloom weaving, there is little industry or other economic activity.

Almost half the population live in *bustees*, or small communities of mud huts clustered between the more formal buildings, and the poorer people are mainly employed in domestic service, casual labour, petty trading and informal transport with rickshaws and handcarts. They serve the better-off professional population, and the city is also a trading centre for the surrounding agricultural area.

There are a number of banks in Cuttack, and the national commercial banks are well represented there, but the city is unusual in that its fastest growing bank, with the largest number of individual customers, is the Cuttack Urban Cooperative Bank (CUCB). The largest bank in the city in terms of the volume of deposits is the State Bank of India, but this is only because of its virtual monopoly of government banking business.

The CUCB is the most profitable cooperative bank in Orissa, and one of the most successful in all of eastern India. Most of the cooperative banks in the region have become heavily politicised and are burdened with massive accumulated losses and non-recoverable loans. The CUCB, however, has resisted interference of all kinds, and is growing at a rate of over 30 per cent per year. The Reserve Bank of India has recently allowed urban cooperative banks to open branches in nearby small towns which do not have their own cooperative banks, and to service customers who reside up to ten km beyond their city limits. The CUCB is taking advantage of these new opportunities, and plans to open new branches in a number of nearby towns.

One of the most important ways in which the CUCB reaches out to new customers, particularly those who are unfamiliar with formal financial institutions and have modest resources, is through its team of about two hundred self-employed collection agents. They offer a daily deposit and loan repayment service, at the customer's place of work, and each one can deal with a hundred or more customers. Mr. C.C. Haldar and Mrs. S. Subalaxmi are typical of the over ten thousand small business people whom the bank serves in this way.

Mr. Haldar runs a roadside stall selling children's dresses, about two hundred metres from the College Square Branch of the CUCB. He started his business in 1990 with Rs. 1,500 of his own savings, and he realised from the very beginning of his business career that he would do more business if he could buy a wider selection of sizes and designs. He was therefore very interested when a collection agent from the CUCB approached him in 1991 and suggested that he might take a loan.

He had never had an account with a bank before, and he knew that their branches were usually closed at the times when it was possible for him to leave his stall, and that it took a long time to make deposits; he had never even considered taking a loan from a bank. The agent explained that the CUCB required new borrowers to start by making regular daily savings; after two or three months, when they had shown that they could manage to put aside a few rupees every day, and had accumulated more than Rs. 1,000 in savings, they could apply for a loan of up to Rs. 5,000.

The agent said that he would call on Haldar every day, or every two or three days at most, at his stall, to collect his savings or repayments. The only time he would have to go to the bank would be to open his savings account and then to receive a loan. Haldar's sales at that time were about Rs. 5,000 a month, and he thought he could save Rs. 10 a day.

The agent took him to the College Square branch of the CUCB and helped him to open a savings account into which his daily savings would be paid. He explained that he would earn 4.5 per cent annual interest on this account, and that the cost of the daily collection service was borne by the bank.

The agent called on him regularly as he had promised, and after three months Haldar had saved Rs. 1,000. He walked down to the branch and paid five rupees for a loan application form. By that time the collection agent had become quite familiar with his business, and he helped Haldar to fill in the simple one page form. He also explained that the loan repayments would have to be guaranteed by two people in case Haldar failed to repay on time. Two nearby traders, who knew Haldar quite well, were already borrowing from the CUCB, and they were willing to sign his form. Borrowers were also required to become members of the Cooperative, and to buy shares to a value of 5 per cent of what they wished to borrow.

Haldar applied for a loan of Rs. 5,000; he was told that the CUCB preferred to disburse loans direct to borrowers' suppliers, rather than in cash, particularly to first-time borrowers, and he therefore obtained a quotation from his Calcutta supplier for Rs. 5,000 worth of dresses.

A member of the branch staff came to inspect his business, in order to make sure that it was as described and that Mr. Haldar was indeed a serious businessman. The collection agent was not allowed to play any part in the loan approval process, since his function was only to collect cash from customers. The visit report was favourable, and the loan was approved by the branch manager and passed to the monthly meeting at head office.

Within a month of getting the application form, Mr. Haldar was asked to go to the branch, with his two guarantors. He was asked to convert his savings account into a term deposit account, which he could not withdraw until his loan was repaid. This account would earn interest at 14.5 per cent a year. He also had to sign a paper authorising the bank to take repayments from this account, and to take possession of his stocks, if he himself did not repay on time. He and the guarantors signed the loan agreement, and a few days later he was given a bankers' draft in favour of his Calcutta supplier for Rs. 5,000. He went to Calcutta soon afterwards, and his business benefited at once from the larger range of stocks that he was now able to purchase.

The loan could be repaid over three years, but the bank staff explained that the interest charge of 13 per cent per year was calculated monthly on the actual balance outstanding, so borrowers could save money by repaying earlier if they wished. Mr. Haldar did not understand the details of interest charges, and soon forgot the figure of 13 per cent; he did remember, however, that he could borrow a larger amount if he repaid the first loan regularly. Because his business was doing well, he managed to repay the first loan in little more than a year. He then borrowed Rs. 12,000, which he also repaid in a year, and in 1994 he borrowed a third loan of Rs. 20,000. This took 18 months to repay, and because of some personal and business problems his repayments were not always regular. The bank therefore advised him to reduce his borrowing, and he took a fourth loan of Rs. 15,000 in 1994.

In October 1996 he was still repaying this at the rate of Rs. 20 a day, every day. He goes to Calcutta twice a month to buy new stocks, and his monthly sales are around an average of Rs. 8,000, depending on the season. His margin is about 40 per cent, and after paying Rs. 100 a month to the local group who control the right to occupy roadside sites, and Rs. 180 for each of his two trips to Calcutta, he earns between Rs 1,000 and Rs. 2,000 a month from his business. He has about Rs. 15,000 worth of stocks, and he maintains a savings deposit account of Rs. 6,000 in the CUCB, as well as his share capital of Rs. 1,000.

Mrs. S. Subalaxmi has been selling bananas from a small roadside stall near College Square in Cuttack for about thirty years. She took her first loan from the CUCB in 1989, for Rs. 5,000, and since then she has taken and repaid four more loans, the last three being for Rs. 10,000 each. She has repaid each loan in little more than a year, and plans to continue borrowing at this level. Before she took her first loan, she used to buy rather small amounts of bananas, and she would sometimes get one week's credit from the wholesale suppliers, but they used to demand one or even two rupees per hundred extra for this service. Mr. Subalaxmi knows nothing of interest rates, but she is sure that her loans from the CUCB are less costly.

She now buys about Rs. 5,000 worth of bananas twice a week. Her husband also has a banana stall elsewhere in the city, and she sometimes finances his purchases as well as her own. He does not sell as many bananas as she does, and she effectively controls his business by limiting the amount of finance she provides. Her loans from the CUCB have enabled her to do this, as well as to increase her own business, and thus to ensure that the family finances are better managed.

K.N. Malik has been a collector for the College Square branch of CUCB since 1991. He was 24 years old at that time. After finishing college he had invested Rs. 25,000 in a garment shop, but his business failed because he selected the wrong stocks and there was too much competition. He knew that it would be virtually impossible to find a job, since there were so many educated unemployed youths in Cuttack, and he enjoyed the freedom of being self-employed, so he decided to apply to the CUCB to be a cash collection agent.

The Bank made some enquiries about him, and they told him that he would have to deposit Rs. 14,000 in a savings account with the Bank, which he could only withdraw if he ceased to be a collector; the Bank demanded this in order to prevent collectors from absconding with clients' money. Fortunately his family owned some property, and they were able to provide the money from the rent which they received.

Malik now collects around Rs. 300,000 a month, from almost 250 clients; the majority of his clients are borrowers rather than savers, since daily collection savings accounts only earn 4.5 per cent annual interest, and clients who can save prefer to have long-term deposits which earn far more. He calls on his clients every two or three days, or daily if they prefer. and he is paid 3 per cent of what he collects, or an average of Rs. 9,000 a month. He has to add 10 per cent of this to his non-withdrawable deposit with the Bank, but this earns 12.5 per cent interest a year. The deposit now totals Rs. 32,000, and Malik thinks that he may one day use this money to start a business again; he has learned a great deal about small business management from his regular contact with clients.

His net earnings of around Rs. 8,000 a month are around twice what his friends who are employed with government or private firms are able to earn, even after paying the costs of the scooter which he has to have in order to get round all his clients. He has to work very hard; each day he has first to go to the bank to pay in the previous day's collections, and then he goes round his clients for at least eight hours, six days a week, but he enjoys the job. He tries to increase his earnings by introducing the services of the CUCB to new clients whenever he can, since he is not allowed to 'poach' clients from other collectors.

The CUCB has 16 branches, 20,000 members and 350 staff as well as the 200 self-employed collectors. Its customer deposits in October 1996 were over one billion rupees, and the loans outstanding amounted to around 900 million rupees. The annual profit was ten million rupees, after allowing twenty million for possible bad debts; 82 per cent of loan repayments were made on the due date, unlike most cooperative and indeed many commercial banks whose on-time recoveries were below 50 per cent and whose potential loan losses were unknown.

The CUCB has successfully resisted political pressure; although two of its ten directors are government appointees, the Bank has never had to take any government shareholding, and has thus retained its independence. The Chief Executive has held the job for twelve years, and is regularly re-appointed by the members at the annual meetings. The staff are treated well, but any who perform badly or break the rules are instantly dismissed; the staff are proud to work for the Bank and, again unlike other banks, there are few labour disputes.

The College Square branch has 35 staff and 10 collectors. Of the 1,600 borrowers, 960 are small business people such as Mr. Haldar and Ms. Subalaxmi, who make their repayments to collectors such as Mr. Malik. Many of them earn their living pushing trolleys around the nearby wholesale market, which they have bought with Rs. 5,000 loans from the CUCB. The loans to these small borrowers total 1,400,000 rupees, or 22 per cent of the total amount outstanding from the branch, and because of the regular collection service only 15 per cent of the total overdue loans for the branch are from this group. The manager does not hesitate to call on the guarantors if a borrower's loan is not repaid on time, and they are usually successful in persuading the defaulter to pay, if only because they know that they themselves will not be able to borrow again if a loan which they have guaranteed is in arrears.

The Bank charges higher interest rates on larger loans; small borrowers such as Mr. Haldar and Ms. Subalaxmi pay 13 per cent, and the rate goes up to 17.5 per cent for loans over Rs. 200,000. This is in conformity with the Government's long-standing policy of requiring the banks to cross-subsidise smaller borrowers from the profits on larger loans, which has recently been relaxed as part of the liberalisation policy. The management of the CUCB do not propose to change the rates, however, even though they are now allowed to. They believe that a cooperative bank should try to serve its poorer members, and they know from experience that today's small borrowers are tomorrow's larger ones; the see the daily collection service as a 'loss leader' which develops new customers and sustains the long term growth of the Bank.

The financial performance of the branch is summarised in the following simplified figures (in rupees):

Simplified Balance Sheet on 31.3.96

Assets		Liabilities	
Cash	100,000	Members' shares	Rs 10,000,000
Advances	62,990,000	Deposits	97,813,500
Surplus lent to head office	44,723,500		
Total	107,813,500	Total	107,813,500

Simplified Profit and Loss Account for Year Ending 31. 3. 96

Interest on Advances, average 15 per cent		14,672,000
Income from other services		2,332,000
Total Operating Income		17,004,000
Plus Interest from HO @ 12 per cent		5,367,000
Total Income		22,371,000
Interest paid on deposits	4,667,000	
Operating Costs	13,751,000	
Provisions	700,000	
Total Costs	19,118,000	
Branch Profit		3,253,000

(Note: This case study was written with the help of Mr. Ramesh Naik, Manager, College Square Branch, Cuttack Urban Cooperative Bank.)

(The exchange rate is approximately Rs. 35 = $ 1.00.)

Comments and Questions

The record of cooperative businesses of any kind is generally bad, although there are many notable exceptions. They are fundamentally difficult to manage, because of the numbers of decision makers and the often conflicting interests of customers, members and staff. Their natural weaknesses have been compounded because cooperatives have been used as instruments for government control and the delivery of subsidy, and they have thus lost credibility as autonomous enterprises.

This case study is about one of the exceptions. This bank has evolved a system of service for micro-enterprises from which any institution, and not just cooperatives, can learn, and it may demonstrate that a cooperative has to be run like any other business, whose shareholders have little or no say in management.

Very large micro-finance institutions, like the Grameen Bank in Bangladesh, are themselves substantial employers, but the micro-finance industry is not normally regarded as a direct form of job creation. The CUCB, however, has been able to design an apparently very effective delivery system which also provides well paid employment for several hundred educated young people. This is a major achievement in itself.

There are, however, a number of questions which the case suggests, including the following:

1) Does the CUCB make a profit from the deposits and loans it generates and services through its commission agent system ? If not, or if the profit is inadequate, how could it be increased ?

2) Borrowers have to maintain savings, and share capital, as a condition of borrowing. Is this necessary, or could the amounts be reduced, in order to avoid what is effectively, lending people back their own money ?

3) What difference, if any, does its cooperative status make to the CUCB, or to this particular part of its operations ? Would a shareholder owned profit-maximising commercial bank be likely to act in the same way, or how might it differ ?

4) Only quite well-off people can afford to be commission agents because of the deposit that is required. Is there any way in which these opportunities might be extended to people who do not have the necessary capital ?

5) Is a daily collection system of this kind only workable in a densely populated urban area, or are there ways in which a similar system might be used in rural areas ?

CHAPTER 13

MASOKO MADOGO MADOGO MARKET SOCIETY, DAR ES SALAAM, TANZANIA

A group of about seventy market stall operators in Temeke District of Dar es Salaam set up the Masoko Madogo Madogo, or 'little market society', on the first of January 1976. Some of them sold fruit or vegetables, others sold fresh or dried fish, and there were also some butchers. Each trader tended to specialise in one or two items, such as green bananas, onions or one kind of fish, so that there was little direct competition and as a group they provided nearly everything that local people needed. They operated from a piece of vacant land in the Tandika Kwamaguruwe area of Temeke District of Dar es Salaam, and their objective in starting the society was to build up capital from which they could obtain loans for themselves. They made small regular contributions to their shares in the common fund, and individual members could then borrow from the fund when necessary.

At that stage of Tanzania's history any joint activity of that type had to be registered as a cooperative society, and they finally obtained their registration in February 1978. Their official status then enabled them to acquire a formal forty year lease from the City authorities for the land where they operated. The cost of this was nominal, but they had to agree to construct a supermarket on the site in order to secure the lease and to ensure that it was extended. The City Council used this device to ensure that the city would be developed according to their plan, but it was not clear by what date the supermarket would have to be built, or what would actually constitute a supermarket for the purposes of securing their lease.

During the next twenty years the Society continued to run its lending scheme. Members' contributions were not always regular, and the value of their savings was seriously eroded by the three-figure annual inflation which took place during the 1980s. The group used its own members' savings, and from time to time they also took loans from government schemes as they became available; these included two loans from the

Tanzania Youth Development Fund, which were taken by sub-groups within the Society as the Fund demanded.

The Society also took on other functions. They constructed some market stalls for rent to non-members, and a common toilet. Some members who were in the same line of business also used the Society as a way to hire vehicles for transporting their goods, and for joint purchase of supplies, and the Society employed a guard to look after members' stalls at night.

Members agreed, however, that the most important benefit they gained from their membership of the Society was the right to occupy the land. As the city grew, and as the economic structural adjustment process encouraged large-scale private investment, there was more and more pressure for land. Informal business people like themselves were often forced by the authorities to vacate the places where they had done business for many years, but because the Masoko Madogo Madogo were formally registered and had a lease to their land, they were able to stay where they were.

They had built a small office and a few permanent shops for butchers who needed them, but the majority of the members still operated from the same temporary shelters of poles, rusty corrugated iron sheets and plastic with which they had started. They could not afford anything better, and this was in any case what they and their customers were used to.

They did face some pressure from the authorities, because they had not built a proper supermarket, and a wealthy businessman who occupied the next site tried to claim their land because it had not been developed as it should have been. The Society eventually settled this by handing over part of the land they were not using to the businessman, in return for an informal undertaking from him and the authorities who had supported him that they would not pursue the issue. The members agreed that they would have been unable to deal with this and similar claims if they had not been able to act jointly and defend their case through legal channels as well as through informal pressure.

In 1991 the Society made some loans to some non-members who operated near to their site and who rented their stalls from the Society, but some of them failed to repay, and there was no way in which they could be compelled to do so. The members decided in future only to lend to one another. Borrowers were only allowed to borrow up to twice their accumulated savings. Prospective borrowers were also required to be a member of a sub-group who would agree to guarantee their loans, but sub-group members were not allowed to 'club' their savings so that members who wanted to borrow more than twice their own savings could borrow against the savings of those who were not borrowing.

The cooperative regulations under which the Society had been established in 1978 limited the interest rate they could charge on their loans to ten per cent. The regulations were not clear as to how this should be calculated, but the Society adopted a simple approach; they set a maximum loan period of ten months, and borrowers had to repay whatever amount they had borrowed plus ten per cent, regardless of whether they repaid their loans in regular instalments or in a lump sum at the end of the period.

They also added a further five per cent penalty interest on loans that were not repaid within the ten month maximum period, and there were occasions when this penalty was imposed. In a few cases the Society also took possession of the simple materials from which non-payers' stalls were constructed. This effectively prevented them from operating, so they either paid up or left the Society.

In late 1993 the Masoko Madogo Madogo were approached by a staff member of a German-assisted project which had been set up to assist groups such as their own. This project was run in collaboration with SIDO, the Small Industries Development Organisation, which had itself been established by the Tanzanian Government in 1973 in order to assist small industries in the country. SIDO had concentrated its work on formal small industries, rather than on very small or 'informal' enterprises such as the members of the Masoko Madogo Madogo, and had provided these industries with loans, equipment, training, premises and other services.

By the 1990s SIDO was in deep financial trouble, like many similar industrial development institutions in Africa and elsewhere. Many borrowers, particularly those with political connections, had not repaid their loans, much of the organisation's equipment was broken down, and foreign donors and the Government were reluctant to continue to support it.

Senior management of SIDO, and the German development agency, GTZ, felt that their new approach of working with self-help organisations would assist in the process of linking SIDO to the enormous numbers of people who by then had to make their living from micro-enterprises, like the members of the Masoko Madogo Madogo society. These people needed help, and it was also felt that they might eventually become paying customers for SIDO's other services, such as training, loans and so on.

Most of the groups with which the SIDO/GTZ staff worked were not registered societies, and had been established far more recently than the Masoko Madogo Madogo, as more and more people were compelled to start informal businesses in order to survive. Like the Masoko Madogo Madogo, however, the main reason for their existence was usually to protect their places of work. Few of them had any formal right to their land, and they relied heavily on joint activity to maintain themselves against pressure from the authorities and private interests who wanted to remove them from the roadsides and vacant lots where they operated.

The SIDO/GTZ representative explained to the Masoko Madogo Madogo's members how he and his colleagues would be able to help the Society to organise itself more efficiently, to maintain better records and so on, and how they would also be able to offer simple training to such of the members who wanted it. The assistance followed a clearly structured approach of so-called 'sub-projects' covering particular functions, and client groups had to pay a fee of around 10,000 Tanzania shillings, or $ 16, for each component. This only covered a small proportion of the cost, but it was felt that if groups paid for the service they would make good use of it and would ensure that it was relevant to their needs.

After some discussion the members agreed that they would benefit from this process. The project staff first took them through the initial stages of their group-strengthening process. As a result of this they re-introduced a regular cleaning service for the site, and the members soon saw that they were getting some tangible benefit from what had been learned. The advisers also helped the Society to improve some of its systems which had not been maintained over the years.

As a second step, the members then agreed in 1995 that they should buy the SIDO/GTZ project's 'savings and credit sub-project'. Many of the newer groups with which the project staff were used to working were just starting savings and credit systems, as a supplement to their primary site protection task. The Masoko Madogo Madogo Society had of course been operating a savings and credit system for almost twenty years, but they were not satisfied with the repayment rate and at certain times of the year they did not have enough money to lend to all the members who wanted to borrow.

As a result of the 'savings and credit sub-project' the members decided in June 1996 to increase their daily 'share' contribution from five to fifty shillings (about eight US cents), so that there would be more money to lend. This was in addition to the fifty to hundred shillings each member paid every working day for the Society's other services.

The SIDO/GTZ project people also said that they had a small fund at their disposal from which suitable groups could borrow to supplement their own funds, so long as they had been though the project's savings and credit training package and agreed to maintain certain conditions. In early December 1995, the Society decided to borrow 450,000 shillings the equivalent of a little over $ 700, from this fund. At the time this added about one-third to their total funds, which was a welcome addition at the season when customers were buying for the Christmas holidays and the members therefore needed as much capital as they could get.

One difficulty was that the project demanded 50 per cent annual interest. The SIDO/GTZ staff justified this by saying that inflation was running at around 40 per cent a year at the time; the commercial banks were also charging about 30 per cent for far larger secured loans. They argued that it was reasonable to demand 10 per cent more from risky untried borrowers such as the Masoko Madogo Society, who had no collateral security which any bank would accept. At that time none of the over one hundred other client organisations of the SIDO/GTZ project had taken a loan from the project, perhaps because of the high interest rate, but the Project's management did not wish to make their clients dependent on subsidised funds, as the Government used to do.

Some of the older and more traditional members, who believed that such high rates were wrong, or even immoral, were against borrowing on such terms. They realised that whoever borrowed the money would have to pay the cost, and they argued that if the staff of the government cooperative department who audited their accounts noticed that the Society was charging more than 10 per cent interest they would be in serious trouble.

Finally, the matter was resolved; the ten members who particularly wanted the money and who could not borrow from the Society's funds because it was not their turn, agreed that they would pay 60 per cent interest on their loans, of which 50 per cent would go to the SIDO/GTZ project and 10 per cent to the Society. They repaid a total of 656,250 shillings at the end of June 1996, of which 45,000 shillings, or 10 per cent of the loan, was paid to the Society and the balance was returned to the project.

Said Ndevu was one of the men who shared this loan. He had been selling onions and garlic in the market since 1978, and had been a member of the Society ever since he started his business. He borrowed 50,000 shillings from the SIDO/GTZ loan, which enabled him to buy three sacks of onions at a time instead of one. Each trip cost about 1500 shillings, regardless of how many sacks he bought, and he estimated that this saved him around two trips per week. He repaid the loan and interest at the rate of 350 shillings a day for seven months; he was not sure how much interest he had paid, but he was satisfied with the whole transaction.

After the SIDO/GTZ loan had been repaid, the members did not borrow money from the project again. Some of the borrowers had had difficulties in repaying such large amounts, although all had paid in the end. The members were also still nervous about breaking the old 10 per cent rule, and for most of the year the Society had more than enough money in its account to satisfy every member who wanted to borrow and who had enough savings to cover half of what he wanted to borrow.

Miss Catherine, the only woman among the 87 active members of the Society, started her vegetable business in the market in 1996. She had been a nurse but had been retrenched as part of the government's economic restructuring programme, and she used her gratuity of 120,000 shillings to buy out an old member who wanted to retire. She hoped that she might be able to borrow from the fund in due course, but in February 1997 she had more than enough working capital to satisfy her customers. If she bought more stocks, they would just remain unsold and be wasted.

Saloum had been selling fruit and vegetables at the same place even before the Masoko Madogo Madogo was set up. He borrowed money for the Society from time to time, but he did not take a loan from the SIDO/GTZ money because of the high cost. He did borrow 45,000 shillings in June 1996 from the Society's own fund, and used the money to buy three extra sacks of potatoes at 15,000 shillings a sack. He sold them in about a week for 17,500 shillings each, and finally repaid the loan, plus interest of 4500 shillings, in October.

The Society kept accurate daily records of all transactions, and each member had a passbook which contained details of his accumulated 'share' contributions to the loan fund, as well as the balance outstanding on any loans. Their repayments, along with their share contributions, which could not be withdrawn unless they left the Society, and their daily fees for services, were all banked in the same current account at the nearest branch of the National Bank of Commerce, which was about five miles away. This did not earn any interest, and although the Bank was paying almost 30 per cent interest on three-month deposits they did not want to tie their money up that long. They also tried to maintain a cash balance of around 50,000 shillings, in order to pay the guard and be able to lend money to any member who unexpectedly needed a small sum.

The Society did not regularly prepare a balance sheet or profit and loss account, since these statements were only required by the Cooperative Department and were normally prepared by their auditors on an occasional basis. In February 1997, however. the financial position of the Society was estimated to be approximately as follows (figures in shillings):

Assets		Liabilities	
Loans outstanding to 63 members	1,375,000	Members' shares	450,000
Cash	70,000	Advance loan repayments	2,000
Bank balance	646,000	Accumulated surplus	3,789.000
Furniture	150,000		
Buildings	2,000,000		
Total	4,241,000	Total	4,241,000

About ten of the 63 borrowers were in arrears with their repayments, for a total of about 400,000 shillings. The remaining loans were fully up to date, and the Secretary was sure that the defaulting members would pay up their dues when the officers threatened to seize their share savings or their equipment, or even to expel them from the Society altogether.

They estimated that the remaining 21 years of the lease, if it could be sold, would be worth several million shillings, but this was purely a notional figure since the lease could not legally be transferred and even if it could it was most unlikely that the members would want to deprive themselves of the place where they earned their living. The buildings were valued at what they had cost to build, including additions and major repairs, so the 'accumulated surplus' item of their balance sheet was not inflated by increases in its value.

In 1997 there were eight borrower sub-groups, which included all the active members, although some of them rarely if ever made use of the facility. These were mainly the more successful members for whom the small loans they could borrow from the Society were insufficient; they felt that it was worthwhile to continue paying the fifty shillings a day required contribution to their savings in order to maintain the solidarity of the Society, on which their continued occupation of the site depended, and also to help their less fortunate comrades.

They, like all the other active members, also paid an additional daily fee of either fifty or a hundred shillings a day whenever they operated their businesses, to cover the cost of the night guard, the rubbish removal service and some small allowances for the Chairman, the Secretary and the Treasurer. The Society also employed a girl to keep their accounts, and members' contributions were used to cover her salary.

The income of the Masoko Madogo Madogo varied according to how many members paid their daily fees, since they did not pay if they did not come to the market. The outgoing payments for officers' allowances and travel, the guard, the cleaning service and their clerk, were more predictable, but they also faced unexpected expenditures, such as legal costs or the fees for the SIDO/GTZ services.

Very approximately, however, their income and expenditure for January 1997, a typical month, was as follows:

Income (in shillings):		
Members' fees for guard		108,000
Interest on loans		14.000
Rent for stalls		76,000
Members' payments for joint purchases and transport		57,000
Total		255,000
Expenditure (in shillings):		
Cost of guard, fence maintenance, site cleaning, officers' allowances etc.	115,000	
Expenditure on maintaining rented stalls, and on joint purchases and transport	62,000	
Total:	177,000	
Monthly surplus		78,000

The officers of the Masoko Madogo Madogo felt satisfied with their Society. Unlike many cooperative societies in Tanzania, they had not been hijacked by political interests, and they did not have any outstanding debts. The daily contribution 150 shillings amounted to around 10 per cent of the daily earnings of some of the poorer members, and the fact that they were willing to pay this much suggested that they thought that they were getting good value for their money.

(The exchange rate is approximately 625 Tanzania Shillings = $ 1.00.)

Comments and Questions

The Masoko Madogo Madogo is a cooperative enterprise, like the Cuttack Urban Cooperative Bank, but of a very different type. The cooperatives in Tanzania have been misused more than in most countries, and to have remained active, solvent and even profitable over twenty years is in itself a great achievement.

The lending operation is only a small part of the Society's activities, which are more related to property rights and security, but it is important, particularly for some members, and it appears there is some unsatisfied demand; more members would take loans, for higher amounts, if funds were available.

The members and the officers themselves also believe it to be a profitable part of the whole operation, which means that it should be retained and expanded for the good of the Society as a whole.

It is always difficult for the owners of any enterprise, and particularly a small one, to know which products or activities are profitable and which are not. Carpenters often put great effort into making items whose price barely covers the cost of materials, when other products can earn them a good return for the labour as well as paying for the timber, and multipurpose service organisations such as the Masoko Madogo Madogo have the same problem. This can in itself be an argument in favour of concentrating on one activity, as many successful micro-finance organisations do, but this would not be appropriate for this group. They should therefore try to assess the economics of each service, in order either to eliminate or at least to be aware of cross-subsidy.

In a general sense, however, this case demonstrates the resilience of institutions. The Society survived for 20 years, in spite of misdirected assistance programmes, hyper-inflation and changing circumstances, because it satisfied a genuine need of its members. Credit was not the main need, and the Masoko Madogo Madogo might have survived as well without it, but it probably provided a form of 'glue' to retain members' commitment when the threat of dispossession seemed to disappear. Regular savings, even without the possibility of loans, can keep a group together so that it is ready to perform more vital functions when necessary; this may have been the major role of the loan facility of the Masoko Madogo Madogo.

Questions

1) Why did the other client organisations of the SIDO/GTZ project not make use of its loan facility ? Was the interest rate too high, or the conditions too strict, or was there no need for loans at all ?

2) Was the SIDO/GTZ project right to offer loans to its client organisations ? Should a technical assistance and training project offer loans at all ?

3) Was the Masoko Madogo Madogo's lending scheme profitable ? If not, how could it have been made profitable, without reducing the quality of the service to members, and perhaps by enhancing it ?

4) How might the Society have improved its method of charging interest on loans ? Did the inaccuracies inherent in the present method really matter to the members, and how can correct calculations be reconciled with simplicity and flexibility ?

5) In a cooperative financial enterprise, does it matter if some services cross-subsidise others, even if nobody is aware of the fact, so long as all the members are willing and able to benefit from the services as and when they need them ?

CHAPTER 14

THE PINGUA BRANCH OF DHENKANAL GRAMYA BANK, ORISSA, INDIA: 'LINKAGE' TO SELF HELP GROUPS

Pingua is a large village of about 10,000 people of the area in Dhenkanal District of Orissa State of India. It is the trading centre for a large but thinly populated and very poor area. The total population of the area is around 25,000 in some twenty-five villages. There is very little irrigation and most of the people are subsistence farmers, who depend on the erratic rainfall to cultivate rice, groundnut and some other crops.

There are two banks in Pingua. One is a branch of United Commercial(UCO)Bank, one of the large nationalised banks which dominate commercial banking in India. The Pingua branch of this bank, however, is burdened with heavy overdues from 'sponsored' government loan programmes, and a notice is displayed in the branch saying that their current rate of recoveries is only about 50 per cent; until this is improved, the bank will not be making any loans at all.

The other bank is a branch of the Dhenkanal Regional Rural Bank, which is one of the 196 rural banks which were established by the Government of India in around 1980 in an effort to improve the provision of financial services to rural people, and particularly to the poor. By 1997 about 90 per cent of these banks were technically bankrupt; their share capital had been eroded by continuing operating losses, since the 'spread' between their cost of money and the low rates of interest which they were allowed to charge was far too low to cover their costs.

To make things worse, the banks had until 1995 only been allowed to make loans to their nominated target groups, which were basically the rural poor, and most of these loans were under government 'schemes'. Many of these involved large subsidies and other attractions which meant that the borrowers had usually to be sponsored by government officials. This inevitably led to some syphoning-off of the proceeds, and borrowers who had only received a proportion of their loans or subsidies were naturally reluctant to repay.

Finally, in 1990, the Government ordered the banks to waive repayments on all overdue small loans to rural borrowers. The banks were eventually compensated for the losses, but whatever remained of a 'credit culture' in rural India was destroyed. The Regional Rural Banks suffered the most, since their customers came almost entirely from the groups who were most affected by what had happened.

The Indian economy had since independence been managed with heavy controls and massive subsidies, along with the even heavier concealed costs of the recurring losses incurred by public enterprises, such as the Regional Rural banks. In 1991 the country faced an economic crisis, and it became clear that this system was no longer tenable. The government was forced to introduce a programme of 'liberalisation', which was not dissimilar to the structural adjustment which so many countries had already initiated.

The situation of the Regional Rural Banks was only one of the myriad of problems which now had to be confronted. Their situation was complicated by their ownership. The Central Government owned 50 per cent of the shares, the State Governments owned 15 per cent and the remaining 35 per cent was owned by a commercial bank, which had been chosen to sponsor each Regional Rural Bank. Each bank had a Chairman who was deputed from the staff of its sponsor bank. Although he was nominally autonomous, there were numerous ways in which the sponsor bank, and representatives of state and central government, could, and did, interfere in day-to-day management.

A great deal depended on the personality of the Chairman, and the policy of the sponsor bank. The Dhenkanal bank was fortunate in that its Chairman had identified himself totally with his new position, and was willing to take independent decisions and even to compete with the Indian Overseas Bank, which was the sponsor of the Dhenkanal Bank, and was also his employer, to which he would return after his three-to-four-year period with the Rural Bank was over.

The financial situation of the Dhenkanal Bank was no better than that of most of the Rural Banks, and its accumulated losses at the end of the 1995/6 financial year amounted to about 90 million rupees, or about two-and-a-half million dollars. Management estimated that the Bank would lose a further ten million rupees during the year ending March 1997, but this loss would be caused by provisions for bad debts which had not been taken previously.

In 1993, as part of the liberalisation process, the government had allowed the Rural Banks to start making larger loans to 'non-target' borrowers, such as traders, transport businesses and other local firms, and in 1996 the limits on their interest rates were removed; they could charge any rate of interest they chose, even on the smallest loans. The Dhenkanal Bank was taking advantage of this new freedom, and the operations for the year 1996/7 were expected to show a small profit, not including the losses from making provisions for previous bad debts. Management had forecast that Bank would make a profit thereafter.

It would obviously take many years before the Bank could earn enough profits to cover its past losses and return to solvency, but the Government had already started a programme to recapitalise the Rural Banks. Preference was given to those which were already demonstrating their capacity to improve their results, and all the staff realised that the very survival of their Bank depended on their efforts.

Like many of the Rural banks, the Dhenkanal Bank mobilised more savings than it made loans. The ratio of credits to deposits for the Bank as a whole was only about 60 per cent, but the Pingua branch had always been different; in early 1997 its equivalent ratio was about 130 per cent. There were very few substantial businesses in Pingua, but the bank had taken full advantage of its new freedom to undertake profitable business with them. The Pingua branch was making a small operating profit by the beginning of 1997; its financial position at the end of February was approximately as follows (in rupees):

Assets		Liabilities	
Cash	100,000	Deposits	16,800,000
Agriculture loans	3,300,000	Savings	3,400,000
Term loans	3,000,000		
Jewel loans	3,400,000		
Other loans	15,100,000		
Interest receivable	1,300,000		
Furniture	1,600,000	Interest accrued	1,800,000
Total	27,800,000	Borrowed from Head Office	4,500,000
LESS provisions	1,300,000		
Total	26,500,000	Total	26,500,000

The operating figures for the eleven months ending 28 February were as follows:

Income:		
Interest on Advances		3,000,000
Expenses:		
Interest paid on deposits/savings	2,200,000	
Interest paid to head office	200,000	
Salaries, rent etc.	500,000	
Total		2,900,000
Profit		100,000

The branch had a total staff of six people, including two clerks and a messenger. There were 3,220 loan accounts and 4,500 depositors, and it was considered one of the more successful branches of the bank.

The Branch Manager was very aware, however, that the mission of the rural banks was to serve the rural poor; although they should take every opportunity to compete with the 'mainstream' commercial banks, the long-term objective should be to provide financial services to poor people in a way that satisfied their needs but was also self-sustaining.

In the past the banks had failed to reach most poor people and had also incurred massive losses; both failings had to be addressed. Many earlier 'schemes', such as the Integrated Rural Development Programme, had failed because they involved a large amount of subsidy, and the beneficiaries themselves had no commitment; the loans were perceived as 'handouts', rather than as commercial transactions. These loans were also uneconomic to handle, because they involved very small amounts.

One new approach, which had the potential both to satisfy people's needs and to be profitable for the banks, was to make loans to self-help groups (SHG), which the groups would then on-lend to their members. The National Bank for Agriculture and Rural Development (NABARD), which was the apex bank through which the government attempted to increase the flow of credit to rural areas, had for some years been promoting this approach. They provided training to bank staff, and they also offered refinance to the banks at the heavily subsidised interest rate of 6.5 per cent; the banks were allowed to charge the groups 12 per cent, and the resulting 5.5 per cent 'spread' was considered sufficient to cover the transaction costs, which were in any case proportionately lower than for loans to individuals, because the bank only had to deal with one loan, to the group, instead of individual loans to each member.

Because the groups had to demonstrate their capacity to save before they could borrow, and the members were all responsible for each other's loans, on-time repayment rates were usually 100 per cent or at least well over 95 per cent. This was in dramatic contrast to the recovery rates of 50 per cent or less to which rural banks had become accustomed. This made loans to self-help groups still more attractive for the bank.

By March 1997 a total of 49 such groups had opened savings accounts with the Pingua branch, and their deposits amounted in total to about Rs. 400,000. Forty five of the groups were exclusively women's groups, and four were men's groups, since it was not normal in this area for men and women to engage in business activities together.

The deposits included about Rs. 150,000 from 16 groups which had received grants from the government under one of the many 'poverty alleviation schemes' which had survived the process of liberalisation. These groups were generally not as cohesive or well-managed as the groups which had accumulated their own money without any grants, and they had often obtained their grants though political influence. Although the Bank was naturally happy to take their deposits, they were not considered good borrowers.

The Bank had extended loans to 7 of the other 33 self-help groups, for a total of Rs. 470,000. The loans were for a period of four years, although the Bank was happy to accept early repayments, and the groups paid 12 per cent interest. The Bank was able to borrow the same amount of money from the National Bank's refinance, at 6.5 per cent interest. Although it was not possible to segregate the cost of dealing with these loans, since they were all part of the Bank's normal business, the Manager thought that the 5.5 per cent spread on the total of the loans, which amounted to almost Rs. 26,000 on an annual basis, was enough to cover all the costs of this small but important part of his branch's business.

The Radhakrishna Samiti was one of the self-help groups which had taken a loan from the rural bank. The group had been in existence for many years as a traditional 'merry-go-round'. or 'chit find'. The twenty women members paid in a certain sum every month and each took the total 'pot' in turn. Sometimes several months had gone by between the end of one such contribution cycle and the beginning of the next, but in November 1994 the group had decided to put their operation on a more regular basis. They did this because the Manager of the Rural Bank had contacted one of their members and had told her that he was now willing to lend money to groups such as theirs. If they could show that they could save regularly, and accumulate a reasonable sum, he could lend them up to three times the amount that they had saved.

The members agreed to save ten rupees a month, but they realised after a few months that it would take too long to accumulate a reasonable amount this way, so they increased their savings to fifteen rupees a month. This was still too slow, and they decided in July 1996 to make a one-off contribution which brought their savings up to Rs. 11,000. The Manager explained that if they put this on fixed deposit in the Rural Bank at an annual rate of interest of 13.7 per cent, they would be able to borrow three times their savings. The group followed his advice, and they borrowed Rs. 30,000 from the rural bank in July 1996.

This loan was repayable at a rate of Rs. 800 a month over three years, including interest of 12 per cent charged on the declining balance. The members agreed that they would themselves pay interest to their group at a monthly rate of 3 per cent on their loans. They settled on this rate because that was what some of them had been used to paying to moneylenders, who also demanded that they surrender their jewellery as security. They were happy to pay the same amount, because they knew the money would go to their own group and not to the moneylender. They could also retain their jewellery, so that they could wear it when appropriate, or use it as security to borrow money elsewhere in emergency.

They took loans for the total amount, and the total of the monthly interest payments paid by the members to the group, at 3 per cent of Rs. 30,000, was Rs. 900. This was sufficient to cover the group's payments of principal and interest to the Bank. They realised that this meant that they need never actually repay their loans. After four years, the Bank loan would all be repaid from their interest payments, and they could retain the principal amounts. Naturally, they were delighted.

On March 12 1997 the financial position of the Radhakrishna Samiti was approximately as follows (in rupees):

Assets		Liabilities	
Bank deposit	10,000	Members' Savings	11,900
Savings Account	1,950	Loan from Bank	26,250
Loans to members	30,000	Surplus	3,800
Total	41,950	Total	41,950

The group meets regularly every month, and the members bring their loan payments as well as the Rs. 15 which they have agreed should be their monthly savings contribution. If any member is unable to make her contribution, the group usually allows her one month's grace, but they also levy a one rupee fine. In addition to their financial affairs, they discuss other things such as the polio vaccination campaign, how to deal with drug addiction and their children's education.

Sunjulota Sahu is one of the members of the group. She adds to her family's income by paddy husking, and her loan of Rs. 1,500 from the group means that she can buy more paddy at one time. She can earn about ten rupees on every hundred rupees worth she buys, after paying for the paddy and the fuel, and the process takes around three days. It does not occupy all her time, and her only alternative source of income is casual labour. She can earn about thirty rupees a day from this work, when it is available, but she prefers to husk paddy at home since she can also take care of her family at the same time.

Sunjulota also uses some of the money for household expenses, and she has so far had no difficulty in paying the monthly interest charge of Rs. 45 on her loan, as well as the regular monthly saving of fifteen rupees. Her only problem is that there is not always enough paddy available, since so many women are now able to buy it, and she would like to find another business in which to invest her money.

The Laxminarayan Group is another customer of the Pingua Rural Bank, which had started by saving and lending in kind rather than in cash. These 20 women had for many years been saving 4 kg of rice each month. They used to allow one another to borrow from their accumulated store when they were in need, and the borrower had to repay whatever she had borrowed, plus three kg per hundred kg per month.

They had changed to cash saving in 1996 when they heard that groups could borrow from the Rural Bank. They sold their rice store for Rs. 7,000, and they then saved Rs. 25 a month each for six months. This brought their total savings to Rs. 10,000. The Group then borrowed Rs. 20,000 from the Rural Bank, and the members borrowed from the Group at the same 3 per cent monthly interest rate that they had used when borrowing rice. They continued to save Rs. 25 a month, as well as repaying their loans.

Many of the members of the Laxminarayan Group had used their money to increase the stocks of their own or their husbands' small shops. They could make a profit of around 30 per cent to 40 per cent on the extra goods they bought with their loans, and they could sell the goods in less than a month. Some members, however, thought that they should start a joint betelnut processing business which the whole group could share. Some of the others did not support this idea, because they wanted more money for their own businesses, but they were all confident that the issue could be resolved amicably by discussion at their regular meetings.

Purunamanga village is one of the very poorest villages in the Pingua area. The 1,000 people who live there are all 'lower caste', and they own only some 300 acres of un-irrigated land between them. Their main source of income is weaving, but the official cooperative society which the Government started for them in the early 1980s generally fails to meet their needs. The Society was originally intended to finance the weavers, but it now acts more like an employer, providing thread and taking back the finished cloth, and allowing a very small margin to the weaver. The Society is dominated by a small group of men with political connections; they mismanage its affairs, and the few benefits it does provide go mainly to this particular group.

Many of the women in the village are weavers, and they feel particularly badly served by the Society. Ten of them came together in 1986 and formed the Mason Tusi Mahila Group. They started by saving Rs. 10 a month, which they later increased to Rs. 20, and by 1996 they had accumulated a total of Rs. 20,000 from their savings and from the interest they paid on the small loans they took from their own savings.

The Manager of the Pingua Branch of the Rural Bank was anxious to spread the Bank's self-help group lending outside Pingua itself. He visited Purunamanga village and identified the Mason Tusi Mahila group as a possible customer. He persuaded them to deposit their Rs. 20,000 with the Bank, at 13.5 per cent interest, and sanctioned a loan of Rs 50,000 to them, at 12 per cent interest, repayable over four years.

Weaving requires substantial working capital, because of the high cost of yarn. One shawl, for example, takes about Rs. 125 worth of material, and can be sold for around Rs. 160. The weaving involves at least one full day's work, but it is particularly difficult for the women to buy the yarn without going through the Society. They, or more often their husbands, have to travel to the city of Cuttack, which takes at least one full day, and they can only buy at wholesale prices if they buy about Rs. 5,000 worth of yarn at one time. It is not difficult to sell the finished products; the main problem is to finance the necessary raw material.

The members have each borrowed Rs. 5,000 from the Bank loan, and they have decided to reduce the interest charge to 1 per cent a month, or the same amount that the Bank is charging them. They feel that 3 per cent on Rs. 5,000, or Rs. 150 a month, would be too heavy a burden, since it would be more than a day's earnings. They are still saving Rs. 20 a month, and they have Rs. 1,000 in cash as well as their fixed deposit with the Bank, but they would like to be able to borrow more money so that each member could take loan of about Rs. 25,000; this would really enable them to put their weaving businesses on a sound footing.

The Branch Manager plans to identify more self help groups, and to encourage them to deposit their savings and to take loans from his Branch. In March 1997 they contributed barely two per cent of the business of the branch, but he was confident that this could without difficulty be expanded to around 20 per cent, and that this would be good business for all concerned. They are profitable customers for the Bank, so far every instalment has been paid on time, and the members of self-help groups are precisely the people whom the Regional Rural Banks were set up to serve.

(Note: This case was prepared with the assistance of P.C. Mishra, Manager, Pingua Branch, Dhenkanal Gramya Bank.)

Comment and Questions

This case is unusual in at least two ways:

First, there are many such groups in India which have borrowed from banks, such as the Mahila Laxmi Sangam which is described in the earlier case, but the majority of the linkages have been facilitated by NGOs, which also continue to assist the groups once they have taken a loan. In this case no NGO is involved.

Second, the Dhenkanal Gramya Bank is a classic example of a bank which has been more or less destroyed by misguided policies. Such banks, if they recover at all, are usually very conservative, but this bank, at least in Pingua, is acting in a very innovative way. Self-help groups are unfamiliar customers, and they are usually introduced by NGOs.

The members of the groups, and particularly the weavers in Purunamanga, are very poor people, Orissa is in many respects similar to Bangladesh, which is not far away, and these women are quite like the members of the Grameen Bank and the BRAC groups described earlier. They are however in this case being served by an ordinary bank, which has no special systems to cope with such groups, and whose customers are mainly better-off people. This is very different from the Bangladesh situation.

The profitability and the economic reality of the whole experience is however substantially distorted by the NABARD refinance. This particular form of subsidy has survived the process of liberalisation, unlike many others, and seems likely to continue. This may or may not be for the benefit of the bank and its clients.

Questions

1) No NGO has been involved in the initiation or development of these groups, nor in the process of linking them to the Bank. What differences, positive or negative, might an NGO have made, to the groups and their membership, and to the Bank ?

2) What rate of return are the members earning on the money they have invested in their enterprises ? What bearing does this have on the interest rates they chose to charge themselves for their loans, and on the rates the bank can charge the groups ?

3) Although the Bank has recently been freed to charge whatever interest rate its management decides, on loans of any size, this only applies to loans made from funds the Bank itself has mobilised from depositors. The on-lending rate for refinance funds obtained from NABARD is limited depending on the borrower; for self-help groups, it cannot exceed 12 per cent. Is this control really in the best interests of the bank and the expansion of loan to self-help groups ?

4) Would the Bank be well-advised to lend to the self-help groups from its own funds, taking a higher spread than the maximum five-and-a-half per cent allowed on the NABARD refinance ?

5) The groups can earn 13.5 per cent on their deposits with the Bank, while they only have to pay 12 per cent on their loans. What are likely to be the effects of this paradox on their attitude to banks, and on the bank's attitude to them ?

6) Do group customers of this sort demand a fundamentally different approach and methods, or can they be fitted into the Bank's customers like any other new market segment ?

7) Some group members want to use all their loans for their own or their families' enterprises, while others want to invest in group enterprises. Which is likely to be the best policy ?

CHAPTER 15

PURI GRAMIN BANK AND DSS BALIPATNA, ORISSA, INDIA

In early 1982 there were serious floods in the flat coastal plains of Eastern Orissa, between Bhubaneswar and the sea. As always happens, the poorest people suffered the most, since their homes were in low-lying areas. The coastal belt of Orissa is fertile and is densely populated and very conservative. Most of the land is owned by traditional upper caste groups, and the majority of the lower caste people still live in abject poverty on the fringes of rural villages. A number of educated young people from the land-owning classes felt that they should try to do something for their less fortunate fellow-citizens; their families had for hundreds of years dominated rural soceity in a traditional way, but the younger generation were motivated to try to take some concrete action to improve the life of the poor.

One such group came up in the village of Balipatna, about 20 km from Bhubaneswar, the capital of the State. They called themselves the Darabar Sahya Sansad (DSS), or People's Literature Association, because they had originally come together to discuss Oriya literature. They gave generously of their time and resources to help the poorer people of Balipatna to reconstruct their homes and rebuild their lives.

After the flood emergency was over, some of the members of DSS decided that they would like to try to make a more permanent contribution. They started a number of small welfare activities for the lower caste or 'untouchable' people in the villages. These included a creche for small children whose mothers were employed as casual labourers on roads and construction sites, health education programmes and training courses on biogas and smokeless stoves. At first the members of DSS donated their own labour and did not need any other resources, but after they had obtained official registration as a society in 1985, they were able to obtain government funding for these programmes.

In 1992 they managed to obtain support from a German voluntary organisation for a one-year programme to train and facilitate the development of women's savings groups in the area. After this had been successfully completed and a number of women's groups had been started, DSS received further support from organisations in the Netherlands, from Norway and from Austria. Thirty women were trained in applique, thirty in coir weaving and ten in dairy farming.

Each of these programmes was successful, in that the trainees were able at least to supplement their incomes with their new skills, and they formed informal groups after the training. Some of them ran their businesses individually, and others, such as those who were keeping dairy cows, sold their products through the new groups. One reason for starting the groups was to be able to access government support, which was not available to individual producers, and several of the groups obtained various grants and other services.

The management of DSS felt that they should adopt a more coordinated approach, since these activities were satisfactory in their own right, but were making little overall impact on the whole community. A few women were benefiting, but there was a need for something which would bring together all the women, regardless of their activities.

Most of the groups which DSS had promoted had started regular savings schemes. The members saved small sums of money, such as two rupees a month, since group saving was a local tradition and some of them had been advised during their DSS training courses to try to accumulate funds for their personal and business needs in this way. By 1994 several of them had opened post office savings accounts; these paid lower interest than bank accounts, but the banks were generally unwilling to open accounts in the name of groups unless they were officially registered. They would not accept accounts in the names of the elected officers, since these would be likely to change annually.

The DSS staff had been trying to identify a bank where these groups might deposit their savings, and from where they might later borrow further money to on-lend to their members. This approach to financial intermediation for poorer communities, and particularly for women, was being vigorously promoted by the National Bank for Agriculture and Development (NABARD), the central financial institution for rural development.

In order to encourage such loans NABARD was willing to provide refinancing loans of 100 per cent of the amount the banks lent to the groups, at the heavily subsidised interest rate of six and a half per cent. The banks could charge the groups 12 per cent, and the resulting 5.5 per cent margin meant that this could be more profitable for the banks than most of their business. NABARD suggested that the banks should base their loans on the amount the groups had saved. No hard and fast rules were laid down, but it was suggested that first loans should be no more than twice a group's savings; when this was satisfactorily repaid, they might proceed to four or even five times. Banks were also free to set the term of the loans as they wished, but three years was recommended to be the maximum period.

Banks were also free to decide whether they should insist on the groups keeping their savings in the bank as security for their loans, or whether they should merely ascertain that the savings had in fact been accumulated, and then allow the groups to retain their own money for on-lending along with the money to be borrowed from the bank. Experience showed that almost all loans to self-help groups were repaid on time, but the banks had to carry the whole risk; the refinancing loans from NABARD had to be repaid regardless.

In spite of this rather generous incentive package, the commercial and rural banks which had actually to implement the idea were very slow to collaborate. They had for many years been compelled to provide subsidised credit to rural people under a variety of government sponsored 'schemes' which had led to enormous losses but had not generally benefited the poorest people, particularly the women. Most bankers were reluctant to lend more money to what they perceived as the same sort of programme, and when DSS approached the manager of the nearest branch of State Bank of India, the biggest bank in the country, they were unable to persuade him to work with their groups, even though they showed him the Reserve Bank circular which specifically authorised it. The manager said that his main task was to try to recover old loans, and he would have to wait until the regional office of his own Bank informed him about the scheme.

At around this time a new manager was posted to the Balipatna branch of the Puri Regional Rural Bank. This branch, like most of the Indian Regional Rural Banks, was suffering from chronic problems of operating losses and massive overdues, but the new manager was committed to the cause of rural development, and was determined to try to improve the situation. He had been to a training course on lending to self-help groups, and he thought that this new approach might be one way in which his branch could both fulfil its social mandate and also improve its financial performance. He therefore made a effort to identify potential groups, and non-government organisations (NGOs) which were promoting them, and he contacted DSS as well as Palli Unnayan Parishad, another NGO in a nearby village which was training women's groups to make coir rope and toys.

The DSS staff were happy at last to find a bank manager who was sympathetic to their work, and they discussed with him the possibility of 'linking' to his branch some of the groups which they had promoted. The Manager approached his head office. They did not share his enthusiasm for lending to these groups, particularly since the Bank had the largest accumulated losses of all the 196 Regional Rural Banks in India and they did not want to try any new experiments.

Eventually, however, the Manager was able to persuade his superiors to allow him to make loans to suitable NGOs, which they could then lend to the groups for them in turn to lend to their members. DSS would have to pay 10.5 per cent interest, and could then charge the groups the same rate of 12 per cent that they could have obtained from the bank had they been allowed to borrow direct. It was clear that the 1.5 per cent margin was in no way enough to cover the handling and administrative costs of DSS, but DSS considered this to be an integral part of their service to their clients. They hoped in any case that this was only a temporary transitional arrangement; the senior staff of the Bank would soon see that the groups were good customers. DSS could then withdraw and the Bank would allow the groups to borrow directly.

DSS suggested that five groups, which had between them a total of about Rs 26,500 savings, should be given loans. The Bank Manager visited the groups; he looked at their books and discussed the women's investment plans with them, satisfy himself that the groups were cohesive and that their members would be able to repay their loans.

These groups were mainly made up of women from traditional activity-based lower castes, and most of their members were engaged in pottery, rice husking, turmeric processing, bamboo basket making and applique handicrafts. They had already been taking loans from their own savings for personal consumption expenses such as food, medicine or clothing. They had agreed with DSS that most of the new money from the bank would be used for so-called 'productive' purposes, and the Bank had to have a list of the main uses, but in fact the members were effectively free to use the money as they wished; what mattered was that it should be repaid on time.

The Bank's headquarters also insisted that the groups' savings should be held on deposit at the bank as partial security. Because the loan was to DSS, the five groups had to transfer their savings to DSS who then deposited them with the bank in DSS' name on a fixed one-year term at 13 per cent interest. DSS made a formal agreement with each of the five groups that it would return their savings to them, plus the interest earned, as soon as they had repaid their loans to DSS. Finally, after all these points had been agreed, the Bank disbursed a total of Rs. 53,300 to DSS on 20 March, 1996. DSS at once passed on the funds to the five groups.

The groups made their early repayments to DSS exactly as scheduled. DSS handed the payments on to the Bank immediately. As a result of this satisfactory experience, both DSS and the Balipatna branch of the Puri Regional Rural Bank were soon able to extend the same arrangement to other groups. In October 1996 the Balipatna branch lent Rs. 31,900 to Palli Unnayan Parishad, for on-lending to five groups, and by March 1997 the Nimapada branch of the Puri Gramin Bank had lent Rs. 10,500 to DSS for on-lending to three groups and the Srimukha branch had lent DSS Rs. 15,500 for another four. The Balipatna branch sanctioned a further Rs. 49,000 to DSS for eleven more groups.

DSS negotiated two loans for a total of almost Rs. 618,000 from the Small Industries Development Bank of India (SIDBI) and another development institution. These two loans were at 9 per cent and 15 per cent interest but DSS was allowed to on-lend them to the groups at 15 per cent and 18 per cent; this higher margin made the transaction much more worth-while for DSS, and SIDBI also gave DSS a one-off grant of Rs. 80,000 to help cover the initial expenses of setting up the lending activity.

One typical group was the Pragoti Shila Mahila Sangha in the Harijan or 'untouchable' colony of Hansapara village. Sixteen women started the group in mid-1995, at the suggestion of a DSS field worker. They each saved ten rupees a month, and in early 1997 they started to make a few small loans to one another from their accumulated savings.

In March 1997 they borrowed Rs. 5,000 from DSS, which DSS itself had borrowed from the Nimapara branch of the Puri Gramin Bank. The group had to deposit half the amount they borrowed with the Bank as part security.

At that time their financial position was approximately as follows (in rupees):

Assets		Liabilities	
Cash	130	Members' savings	3,040
Lent to members	5,000	Loan from DSS	5,000
Savings with Bank	2,500	Surplus	340
Fish pond	750		
Total	8,380	Total	8,380

The members' families owned no land, and the women were only able to earn Rs. 30 a day as casual labour on other people's land for a few months every year. They also earned a little from making muri, or puffed rice, from paddy, but this was always limited because they did not have enough capital to buy the paddy.

Now that they were able to borrow from their own fund, the women could afford to buy more. The experience of Mamata Jena, the President of the group, was typical. She borrowed Rs. 300 to buy paddy and fuel, and was able to sell the rice within seven days for a net profit of Rs. 50. She did not consider the cost of her labour, but there was no other way in which she could have earned money in the time she devoted to rice processing. The group had agreed to charge themselves Rs. 5 a month interest for each hundred they borrowed, but Mamata Jena was happy to pay Rs. 15 a month in order to make a surplus of Rs. 50 a week, or about Rs. 200 a month. She also knew, that the interest was going into their own fund and that it would eventually enable them to be independent of DSS or the bank; this was their long-term ambition.

One of her colleagues in the group borrowed Rs. 200 for share-cropping. She spent the money on seeds, pesticides and fertiliser to plant on a piece of land which belonged to an upper caste man who worked in the city. She expected that the crop would be harvested after three months and that it would be worth about Rs 80; she would be entitled to five-eighths of this, or Rs. 500.

The group had also invested Rs. 750 of their money in a fish pond which they were managing as a joint activity. Their first group venture, a small fruit plantation, had failed when some upper caste people had deliberately allowed their cattle to destroy the seedlings, but since then the Sangha had been recognised as a force in the community; their husbands were supporting them, and a number of young men in the village had followed their example and started a youth club.

The members also planned to start a small consumer shop, since there was nowhere in the village to buy the few groceries they needed. Their experience of working together in the Sangha had made the members confident that they could manage these ventures successfully. Since they had started the group they had successfully pressured the local officials to provide a tube-well for their colony, and to release pensions to some of their members who had been entitled to them for many years. When they first started the group they had had to visit the bank four times before the manager would let them open a savings account; now he was actively seeking them out in their own corner of the village in order to assess their financial needs.

They still maintained their regular savings, and they met every Monday at 9 p.m. Every month one of these meetings was devoted to collecting their ten rupee savings, and loan repayments, and to dealing with new loan applications, On the other days they discussed community issues of mutual interest.

The DSS organiser attended the group's meetings occasionally, but he was more than fully occupied in developing new groups. He had helped all the members of the Sangha to learn to sign their own names, instead of using thumb prints, and they now felt that they could manage their own affairs, without his help. They kept separate records of savings, loans and repayments, as well as a minute book and a record of expenditures. They all looked forward to the time when they would no longer need to borrow from anyone else because their own accumulated savings and interest payments, and the profits from their joint enterprises, would be sufficient for all their needs.

Every link in the total financial chain appeared to be gaining something from this arrangement. The individual members were able to significantly increase their incomes because they could borrow money at reasonable rates, and their Sangha also appeared to be a viable enterprise, in a financial and social sense.

DSS had almost Rs. 100,000 outstanding to almost twenty groups; the 'spread' of 1.5 per cent on this sum was clearly insufficient to cover DSS' costs, but these could for the present be absorbed within the total income of some Rs. 80,000 which DSS received from various donors for its programmes. The management of DSS expected within two years to work with some 200 groups. They were undecided as to whether they should encourage the more mature groups such as the Pragoti Shila Mahila Sangha to borrow direct from the banks, so that DSS would be free to work with other new groups, or whether DSS should itself develop its own banking role.

If they chose the latter option, they felt sure that they could obtain sufficient funding from SIDBI or other sources which would allow them to make a reasonable margin on lending. Eventually they hoped that they might even be able to promote a local women's bank.

The manager of the Balipatna branch of the Puri Gramin Bank was well aware that DSS was only one out of the almost 3,000 loan accounts on the books of his branch, and the total sum outstanding to DSS and PUP for lending to self-help groups was only about one per cent of the total loan portfolio of the branch. Nevertheless, he was sure that it was one of the most profitable parts of his portfolio. The repayments were all on time, the administration costs were far lower than for most loans because the amounts were well over the average amount of Rs. 3,000, and the NABARD refinance allowed the bank a reasonable margin on the business. He hoped, as did the managers of the other branches who had taken up lending for self-help groups, that this new type of business would eventually make up a large share of his portfolio. It would be profitable and secure, and would be wholly consistent with the rural development mission for which his bank had been established.

(Note: This case study was written with the help of Kamalesh Kumar Mohanty, Secretary of DSS, and R R K Nayak, Manager of the Puri Gramin Bank, Balipatna.)

(The rate of exchange is approximately Rs. 35 = $ 1.00.)

Comments and Questions

This case describes a four-way partnership between a bank, an NGO, self-help groups and their members. It also shows what can be done by enterprising individuals; the staff of DSS initiated the groups, and the manager of the Balipatna branch of the Bank overcame the reluctance of his own senior management to allow the funds to flow to the people who needed them.

Early initiatives in micro-finance, as in any new field, depend on committed individuals who are willing to take risks and to struggle against entrenched bureaucracy, but institutional inertia must eventually be overcome by institutional change if the benefits of new methods are to reach significant numbers. It is only natural that the top management of banks which have been weakened by misguided policies should be over-cautious, but they must also recognise and grasp opportunities for change and improvement.

Many development interventions are designed to eliminate 'middlemen' and to enable disadvantaged people to deal direct with suppliers or customers. In this case, an NGO and the self-help group have been inserted between the bank and the final borrower, and each must take some margin to pay for its services. The borrower has to bear the extra cost, but in the circumstances there is probably no other way in which she could have received the service.

The margin allowed to the NGO is also derisory, and is no basis for a sustainable system. If micro-finance is to be a real 'industry', as opposed to a short-term fashion which is dependent on the whims of charity, the costs of every intermediary must be covered. Profits are nothing more than the cost of equity capital; the issue is not whether intermediaries such as DSS should make a profit from their role in micro-finance, but whether their costs are covered; in this case, they are not.

The availability of 'bulk' funds from the Small Industries Development Bank of India (SIDBI) gives the NGO the opportunity to chose; should it attempt to 'put itself out of business' as a financial intermediary by facilitating direct links between the groups and the banks, or should it try itself to become a bank ? Options of this source are characteristic of an evolving industry, and they will encourage the diversity and competition which are needed if the market is to be properly served.

Regardless of the route by which they are getting the money, however, the impact on the groups goes beyond income. There are many definitions of 'empowerment', but the social achievements of the Pragoti Shila Mahila Sangha are clear examples of the way in which micro-finance can help disadvantaged people to achieve social goals.

Questions

1) Should DSS limit its role to that of a facilitator, or should it try to become a permanent intermediary in micro-finance ?

2) Can bankers' reluctance to do business with self-help groups be overcome by training, by compulsion, by positive incentives or by the fear of losing their market, and their jobs, to new intermediaries ?

3) Do financial institutions need to know the purposes for which their loans are to be used by the final borrowers, or is it enough to be satisfied with the management and record of the intermediaries through which they reach the final borrowers ?

4) Should donors be willing to subsidise NGOs' financial intermediation role, or should they expect NGOs to demand a sufficient margin from the banks ?

5) What is likely to be the long-term effect of the subsidised finance that is available from NABARD and from SIDBI ? Will it catalyse the flow of non-subsidised funds to micro-finance, or will it reinforce the perception that micro-finance is not a profitable use of funds ?

CHAPTER 16

BANK RAKYAT INDONESIA — CONTOH UNIT

With a population of 30 million people in less than 50,000 sq km, the Indonesian Province of East Java is a densely populated area with many bustling cities and towns. Nevertheless, the region remains primarily agricultural, with numerous small towns and villages dispersed among carefully cultivated rice fields. One such town is Contoh (not its real name), located about 120 km south of Surabaya, the provincial capital of East Java.

Surrounding the town of Contoh are 24 villages, which together comprise the sub-district of Contoh. Within the Contoh sub-district live about 30,000 families, more than 120,000 people. The vast majority of the population depends on agriculture for its livelihood — either as farmers, or by transporting and/or trading crops. Although rice is by far the largest crop, corn, cassava, sweet potatoes, and other fruits and vegetables are also grown. There is also some small industry, much of it home-based, and trading in coffee, soap, shampoo and other cosmetic goods. About 25 km from Contoh is the district capital of Malang, a hill town established in the late 18th century as a coffee-growing centre.

There are three commercial bank offices in the town of Contoh which serve the sub-district. Two of them primarily serve larger and medium-sized borrowers while the third, Bank Rakyat Indonesia, primarily serves smaller borrowers. In addition to the banks, there are also individual moneylenders who work in the market or offer door-to-door credit. However, the interest rates charged by the moneylenders are usually substantially higher than the rates offered by the banks. By one account, BRI has about 50 per cent to 60 per cent of the market of small borrowers in the area.

Bank Rakyat Indonesia (BRI) is a century-old state-owned commercial bank whose traditional mission was to provide financial services to rural areas of Indonesia. Headquartered in the capital city of Jakarta, BRI is Indonesia's largest bank in terms of total employees and number of banking offices. BRI has 323 branches in Indonesia, located in large cities and district capitals. Under the BRI Branch banking system is an extensive network of local banking offices, or Units.

The Contoh BRI office has been in existence since the early 1970s and is typical of the 3,595 BRI Units, which are usually located in sub-district towns or small commercial centres throughout Indonesia. There are also more than 400 BRI service posts which operate under particular Units in areas where there is not enough volume to warrant opening a Unit. These posts are manned by two people, and are open for one or more days a week; the Contoh Unit does not have any of these posts attached to it.

The Contoh Unit is one of 18 Units under the Malang Martadinata Branch, which in turn is one of 35 branch offices under the Surabaya BRI Regional office. There are six people working in the Unit—a unit manager, two credit officers, two deskmen/bookkeepers, and a teller.

Contoh Unit Customer

Mr. Wasis

One of the Contoh Unit customers is Mr. Wasis. Mr. and Mrs. Wasis live with their three teenage children about 5 km from the Unit. Mr. Wasis sells *bakso*, Chinese meatballs and soup, from a stall in the main market in Contoh. He started selling *bakso* more than ten years ago. Before that, he had tried to develop a fruit trading business. However, he was not happy with the income it was generating, and he did not think he could earn enough from it comfortably to support his wife and two young children.

In 1986, he started selling *bakso* door-to-door in his village. His wife makes the *bakso* every day in their home. To buy raw materials for the *bakso*, Mr. Wasis borrowed 50,000 Indonesian Rupiah (about US $ 20) from an informal moneylender who offered credit door-to-door in his village. He immediately had to repay Rp. 5,000, followed by 30 daily instalments of Rp. 2,000, for a total of Rp. 65,000. When his uncle, a former BRI Unit customer, heard about this loan he recommended that Mr. Wasis go to BRI to get a loan.

Listening to his uncle's advice, he went to the BRI Contoh Unit. The teller directed him to the deskman, who gave him information about BRI's loans. The deskman explained that the BRI Unit System had only one type of loan called 'Kupedes' (an abbreviation for General Rural Credit). He discussed the different terms and requirements of Kupedes loans. Kupedes loans from as little as Rp. 25,000 up to Rp. 25 million were available to support any on-going creditworthy productive activity. Mr. Wasis would have to provide collateral, for which he was prepared to hand over his title deed. His uncle had told him, however, that BRI was willing to accept less formal documents, such as tax bills or receipts, if borrowers did not have title deeds, and they would also accept other fixed or movable assets from borrowers who did not own their own land.

The deskman also explained the various maturity and payment combinations. In contrast to his earlier loan, the term of most Kupedes loans was at least a year. Loans were classified either as working capital or investment, depending on the purpose given in the application; working capital loans were available for a maximum of 24 months and investment loans for a maximum of 36 months. The most common repayment plan required only monthly payments.

Mr. Wasis was told that the interest rate was a flat two per cent per month based on the original balance of the loan. However, if he repaid the loan within a six month period, he received half per cent back, as a "prompt payment incentive". This meant that the loan would actually cost 1.5 per cent per month, on a flat basis. This 1.5 per cent Kupedes interest rate works out to an effective annual interest rate of 32 per cent on a declining balance basis.

After discussing his loan proposal with the unit manager and credit officer, Mr. Wasis was encouraged to fill out a loan application. In addition to requesting basic information (name, address, family status and occupation), he had to give the proposed purpose of the loan, his borrowing history, the amount and terms requested, and a brief description of how the money would be used. Mr. Wasis worked with the unit credit officer to figure out what his loan repayment capacity was, based on his current income and expenses.

A day or two later, the BRI credit officer visited Mr. Wasis' home to get more information about his *bakso* business, the proposed use of the loan, and to see his business. The credit officer was also planning to speak to a village official who could vouch for Mr. Wasis' character. About a week after submitting his application, Mr. Wasis received a Rp. 300 Kupedes loan (in 1987), which he had to repay in twelve equal monthly instalments. Although the stated purpose of the loan was working capital for his *bakso* business, Mr. Wasis also used some of the proceeds to help him buy land for a house. However, as long as he could make his monthly payments on time, the Unit staff did not attempt to dictate, or closely monitor, how he used the proceeds of the loan.

Mr. Wasis had accumulated some savings from selling *bakso* door-to-door, and he used his savings to rent a stall in the Contoh market in the hope of developing a more lucrative business. His business progressed well, and in January 1991 he took out another Kupedes loan for Rp. 1 million in order to purchase a market stand. He paid back this loan in 18 equal monthly instalments of Rp. 75,600, after which he immediately received another loan of Rp. 1.2 million. While once again the stated loan purpose was working capital for his *bakso* business, he used some of the loan proceeds to buy raw materials to build the house in which he presently lives.

Mr. Wasis also opened a savings account at the Unit to safeguard his money. The Unit staff suggested that he open a Simpedes account, which allowed an unlimited number of withdrawals, had a simple procedure for withdrawing money, and offered a competitive interest rate. In addition, as a Simpedes customer he was automatically eligible for semi-annual lotteries held at the Branch level in which motorcycles, television sets, radios, and other prizes were awarded. Between 1990 and 1997, Mr. Wasis used the account regularly — with the account balance fluctuating between Rp. 250,000 and Rp. 2.5 million — for his changing cash needs.

In the ten years since Mr. Wasis has been a customer of the BRI Contoh Unit, he has received six Kupedes loans. At the beginning of 1997, he borrowed Rp. 6.0 million (about US $ 2,400) which he was repaying in 24 monthly instalments of Rp. 346,000. During that same period, his sales grew at least sevenfold and at the time of his seventh loan they averaged about Rp. 200,000 per day. While he still works in the market from about 6 a.m. to 3 p.m. every day, he now employs two relatives to assist him.

Mr. Subaeri

Mr. Subaeri lives in a neighbouring village. He has a small dairy farm about 8 km from the Contoh Unit. He lives in the same village in which he was born and raised, where his parents were rice and vegetable farmers. After marrying, he started a fruit farm in 1981 on non-irrigated land he received from his parents. In order to supplement the rather meagre income he earned from the fruit farm, he also took care of cows owned by other villagers. By 1991, Mr. Subaeri had saved enough money to buy his own cows and start his own dairy farm.

In 1996, when an opportunity arose to buy a calf, a friend suggested that he go to BRI. In May 1996, he borrowed Rp. 1.5 million, which he was to pay back in 18 equal monthly instalments of Rp. 113,300. This was the first time he had ever used the services of a bank and the first time he had ever borrowed money. In addition to purchasing the cow for Rp. 700,000, he used the rest of the loan to repair a cowshed he had made in the back of his house and for working capital for his dairy farm.

Following the purchase of the calf his sales almost tripled, and his income almost doubled. Six months after he received his first loan, Mr. Subaeri decided to purchase an adult cow. In November 1996, he repaid his first loan early and received a second Kupedes loan for Rp. 3.0 million, of which Rp. 2.7 million went towards purchasing the cow. He is repaying this loan in 24 monthly payments of Rp. 185,000.

In total, Mr. Subaeri has six cows, of which three are usually producing milk at any one time. He sells the milk to his village dairy cooperative, which then sells the milk in his village. Although he still maintains his fruit farm, with his dairy farm, he now earns in one month what he used to earn over an entire year from fruit farming.

BRI Unit History, Structure, and Performance

Mr. Wasis' and Mr. Subaeri's loans were just two of the 718 outstanding loans, valued at Rp. 1.5 billion (US $ 640,000), which the Contoh Unit staff managed as on December 1996. Of the Unit's loan portfolio, about two-thirds were classified as trading loans and 20 per cent were for agriculture. In addition, the Unit had more than six times as many saving accounts, which totalled almost Rp. 2.3 billion (US $ 980,000).

The Contoh Unit was among the first BRI Units established when the Unit Banking System was initially developed in order to provide subsidised government credit to rice farmers. In 1973, a network of almost 1,600 BRI Units was established in rural areas of Indonesia to carry out the credit component of the BIMAS fertilizer-intensive rice cultivation programme. By 1983 a total of 3,600 units had been opened. Under the BIMAS programme, the Units were a typical example of targeted subsidised rural finance with little savings mobilisation. They did not charge interest rates high enough to cover their costs, they experienced high default rates and they consequently incurred losses in all but one year from 1970 until 1984.

By the early 1980s, it was clear to policy-makers that the credit component of the BIMAS programme should be discontinued and that the Units would either have to be closed down or fundamentally restructured. Rice cultivation was also becoming proportionately less important to the rural population as they became more prosperous, and there were more opportunities in other areas. At about the same time, the Indonesian Government announced financial reforms which allowed banks to set their own interest rates. The Ministry of Finance encouraged BRI to commercialize the Unit Banking system by setting interest rates high enough to cover the cost of funds, overhead costs and the cost of loan losses, and return a profit. This, followed by BRI's successful efforts at savings mobilisation, led to the creation of one of the most wide-reaching sustainable and indeed profitable rural banking networks anywhere in the world.

Between 1984, when Kupedes loans were first introduced, and the close of 1996, BRI Units had lent out more than Rp. 22,379 billion (or almost US $ 13 billion in constant 1996 US $). Losses were small. The long-term loss ratio of Kupedes loans — the ratio of the cumulative amount due but unpaid, to the total amount due — for that period (1984–96) was only 2.2 per cent.

Each Unit is viewed as a separate profit centre, has separate financial statements, and is expected to cover its costs and earn a profit. In 1996, 95 per cent of the Units were profitable. At the end of 1996, there were 2.5 million Kupedes loans outstanding totalling about Rp. 4,000 billion. BRI Units made an average of over 150,000 loans per month in 1996, with an average loan size of Rp. 2.4 million, or about $ 1,200.

About a quarter of all the borrowers are women, but it is estimated that a somewhat greater proportion of the total amount borrowed is actually used by women because many loans which are taken by husbands, because land is usually registered in their names, are actually used by their wives. When the Village Unit system was introduced, management had considered using some form of group mechanism, but they realised that there was no local tradition of loan guarantees outside the family. They therefore decided to lend only on an individual basis, and the system has maintained this policy since that time.

At about the same time Kupedes was introduced, BRI conducted extensive studies on rural savings potential; shortly thereafter it began pilot savings projects. In 1986, BRI introduced a new savings instrument at Units nationwide. This new savings instruments, Simpedes, was designed to meet customer preferences. With a combination of appropriate products differentiated to appeal to various market segments, and effective incentives and marketing efforts, the Unit Banking System has been remarkably successful in mobilising savings. At the close of 1996, there were more than 16 million savings accounts at the 3,595 Units, representing almost 30 per cent of the total number of savings accounts in Indonesia. These accounts had an average balance of Rp. 440,000, and at the end of 1996 totalled more than Rp. 7,000 billion, or about 3 billion dollars.

Overall, the Unit network deposits are almost double that of the total outstanding loans. The BRI system allows Units with a surplus of savings to deposit excess funds with their supervising branches, while Units with more outstanding credit than deposits can borrow from their supervising branch to meet their loan demand. Fund transfers between the BRI Branches and Units receive interest equal to the 'transfer price', which is set monthly by BRI and is usually slightly above the top savings rate offered.

The organization of BRI Units is purposely kept very simple and transparent. Each Unit has at least four staff — a unit manager, credit officer, deskman/bookkeeper, and a teller. As the business of a Unit grows, additional credit officers, bookkeepers and tellers are added according to predefined activity-based personnel standards, up to eleven staff. Units with more than eleven employees are split into two or more Units. The immediate supervisors of the Units are located at the branch level, with each branch supervising about eleven Units.

The BRI Unit staff are recruited from the area where they work. They are only required to have completed secondary school, but an increasing number now have university degrees. All Unit staff start as deskmen or tellers, and promotions are made from within. When they join, all staff receive a one month basic training course about the Unit products and procedures, at one of the five regional training centres operated by BRI. They receive further training when they are promoted, and the centres train about 7,000 staff every year. Unit staff also receive training on-the-job from their Unit managers.

Staff receive a bonus of 6 per cent of their Unit's annual profit as an incentive, up to a maximum of one- to two-and-a-half months' salary, depending on their position. Since 95 per cent of all Units are profitable, this bonus is received by the same proportion of the staff. In addition, staff are eligible for semi-annual cash prizes for particular Unit achievements, such as savings mobilisation or loan quality, depending on the needs of the Unit system and the BRI as a whole.

The financial position of the Contoh Unit is summarized in the following figures (in Indonesian rupiah):

Bank Rakyat Indonesia — Contoh Unit
Simplified Balance Sheet as on 31st Dec. 1996

Assets	
Cash	20 million
Kupedes Outstanding	1,530 million
Surplus lent to Branch Office	879 million
Other Assets	59 million
Total Assets	2,488 million
Liabilities	
Simpedes Deposits	1,583 million
Other Deposits	695 million
Other Liabilities and Equity	210 million
Total Liabilities	2,488 million

Simplified Income Statement, for the Year Ending 31st Dec. 1996

Interest on Kupedes Loans	535 million
Interest Income from Branch	127 million
Other Income	27 million
Total Income	689 million
Interest Expense	394 million
Operation Expense	99 million
Bad debt reserve	53 million
Total Expense	546 million
Unit Profit	143 million

The figure for operation expenses also includes the cost of branch supervision. The bad debt reserve was calculated on a standard formula of 3 per cent of the current loan portfolio plus 50 per cent of all balances which were overdue up to three months past the final due date, plus 100 per cent of all balances which were more than three months overdue past the final due date. Any loan balances which were more than 12 months overdue were automatically written off.

(Note: This case study was contributed by Patricia Markovich of the Harvard Institute for International Development [HIID], Project Adviser to the BRI International Visitor Programme)

(The exchange rate in December 1996 was about 2,350 Indonesian Rupiah = US $ 1.00.)

Comments and Questions

The BRI Village Unit programme is remarkable for a number of reasons. It is part of a large public-sector commercial bank, it is very profitable, it reaches millions of people and it is not based on any form of group system. These characteristics set it apart from most micro-finance programmes, anywhere.

In spite of the fact that it is the world's largest and most successful micro-finance programme, the BRI village unit system has not been widely imitated elsewhere. There are large numbers of 'replications' of the Bangladesh Grameen Bank, in industrialised and less-developed countries, and the self-help group approach is also being introduced in a many countries as well as India. The BRI receives many visitors from donors and financial institutions, and they make a substantial daily charge for such visitors in order to cope with the amount of work they generate. Although some parts of their approach have been adopted elsewhere, there have been no attempts to 'replicate' the system as a whole.

There are many reasons for this. The system's profitability depends as much or more on savings mobilisation as on loans, while most micro-finance programmes focus on increasing the flow of credit. NGOs are in most countries not allowed to take deposits, so the combination of savings and loans is denied to them. Indonesia is a Muslim country, but many people, and not only Muslims, consider the interest rates charged by BRI to be too high. It would be unacceptable in many countries for a large government-owned bank to charge rates at this level. The actual rates, of course, are no higher than those charged by many of the other institutions described in this book, and are many times lower than the rates many BRI borrowers had to pay to informal moneylenders. The issue is not the necessity or the affordability of these rates, but public perceptions.

It is possible, however, to adopt some elements of the BRI experience without necessarily taking on every aspect. One obvious feature is the strictly commercial approach which is adopted. Prizes and competitions for customers and performance bonuses for staff are normally associated with fast-moving consumer goods like toothpaste or snack foods, but BRI has shown that financial services are also a fast-moving consumer good, and can be marketed in the same way.

The management information system is also designed to show field staff how well they are doing. In particular, the transfer prices for funds are set so as to encourage savings mobilisation but also to make lending highly profitable. It is interesting to compare this with the pricing policy adopted by NABARD in India for their refinance, as described in the previous two case studies.

Questions

1) There are many reasons for the success of the BRI village unit programme. The Units were already established, and needed a new role, interest rates were totally decontrolled, and the national economy was growing fast because of oil revenues as well as good economic management. Do these mean that such a system could not succeed in the absence of these conditions, or are there other circumstances where a similarly massive and profitable programme might be developed?

2) Most micro-finance systems depend on groups, as intermediaries or at least as facilitators and social guarantors. The BRI system has achieved broader coverage, more profitably, than any other system, without using groups at all. Is the emphasis on groups exaggerated, and should their role be critically re-appraised?

3) Are there any features of the BRI Unit system which would be likely to discourage poorer people from applying? If so, how might they be changed in order to allow the system to reach those most in need?

4) One of the two borrowers described in the case study is said to have diverted part of the proceeds of two of his loans to buying material to improve his home. Should a lender try to control or prevent diversion of this kind?

5) There is no element of client participation or membership in the BRI village unit system. Its clients use it for saving and borrowing because they get a good deal, not because of any non-commercial loyalty or commitment. Does this make the system any less successful, in a social sense?

from the operations, but they do not give the complete picture, for a number of reasons. The costs include the salaries and other costs of the

CHAPTER 17

THE START-UP FUND — SOUTH AFRICA

Nozibeli Ntuli lives in Mfuleni, one of the many 'squatter camps', as they are called, on the eastern fringes of the city of Cape Town in South Africa. She lives with her husband and their four young children in a small wooden shack, and they share a common toilet and water taps with several other families. For many years 'black' people like Nozibeli were not allowed by law to live in the nearby 'white' suburbs on the slopes of Table Mountain. Nowadays, these restrictions have of course been removed, but for Nozibeli it would be inconceivable to move out of the squatter camps. She and her husband have to struggle to make ends meet where they are, and the Start-Up Fund has helped her to increase the amount she earns from her various small trading activities.

One of Nozibeli's regular activities is selling grilled chicken along the roadsides near her home. She buys 20 chickens for 14 Rand each, or about three dollars, and sells the cooked pieces for about 20 Rand a bird. The firewood to cook all twenty chickens costs about 5 Rand, and she does this about once a week, so Nozibeli earns about 115 Rand, or about thirty dollars from the twenty birds. She also buys a whole pig sometimes, when the opportunity arises, and after butchering it and cooking the meat she can sell it for almost double the cost of 200 Rand.

Another good business is selling duvets, or bed covers, although this is only possible in winter. Nozibeli buys duvet sets for about 120 Rand each, in cash, and then goes around her own and neighbouring townships selling them for 250 Rand. Her customers cannot afford to pay cash, so Nozibeli takes 50 Rand deposit and two further monthly payments of 100 Rand. She usually gets the money in the end, but this business involves a lot of time first to sell the duvets, and then to collect the money.

There are many similar business opportunities, like selling decorations and pictures for people's shacks, but Nozibeli's problem was that she never seemed to have enough money to buy the goods, whether it was chickens or bed covers. She was sometimes able to use the cash she got from her customers to buy new goods right away, but it was more often spent on household needs, and she could only start again when she had managed to save some more money.

In August 1995 Nozibeli heard that a five-day course for business people like her was being run near to her home, and that it would enable her to qualify for a loan from The Start-Up Fund. She knew that if she had more money to invest in her various business activities she would be able to make more profits, and this Fund seemed to offer her an easy way of getting it. It would also include life insurance, to cover any arrears on loans and to provide her next of kin with a lump sum in case of her death.

She decided to enrol for the course, because she knew that she had no real knowledge of management, and she was happy to pay the ten Rand fee. She was rather surprised to find that there was very little traditional teaching; she worked on her own through a series of eight workbooks in Xhosa, her own language, and the Trainer was only there to answer questions and to encourage people to help others who could not read very well.

The course is known as 'the township MBA', since it aims to provide people like Nozibeli with the basic business skills they need to improve their incomes. She learnt some simple ideas about how to promote more sales, but the most important thing was 'weekly money management'; she learnt how to fill in a simple form each week which showed her how much money she would need to keep her business going, and how much she could afford to spend on food and so on.

After she had completed the course the trainer explained that in order to qualify for a first loan of 300 Rand from the Start-Up Fund Nozibeli would have to deposit 100 Rand into a fund known as the Group Indemnity Trust (GIT). This deposit could be reclaimed if she decided to withdraw from the Start-Up Fund system, so long as her repayments were up to date. She was also given a letter to the First National Bank, asking them to allow her to open an account with them, but without any initial deposit; her loans would then be paid into this account, electronically, as she became eligible for them.

When she had done this, Nozibeli filled in a simple one-page form. She only had to give her name and address, the name and address of whoever she chose as the insurance beneficiary and the details of her new bank account. As far as her business was concerned, she had only to state whether or not she was already in business, and to state what type of business it was.

The trainer also explained that she would only receive 300 Rand, although she would have to repay a total of 600 Rand, over six months, to clear her first loan. One hundred and fifty Rand of the extra amount would go into the GIT, to cover her own or any other defaults; unlike her own initial deposit of 100 Rand, this was not refundable. A further 140 Rand would be paid to the Start-Up Training Trust (SUTT), to cover the costs of her township MBA course, and the rest would go to cover the cost of the Start-Up Fund (3 per cent a month). She would have to make the repayments in cash to First National Bank, who would at once credit them to the Start-Up Fund.

Nozibeli was not quite sure how much of her repayments she should consider as interest and how much as payment for other services, but she did know that loan sharks in the township would make you repay 50 Rand interest if you borrowed 100 Rand for only a month. A loan from them for 300 Rand for six months, which was effectively what she was getting from the Start-Up Fund, would thus cost 150 Rand a month, or 900 Rand for six months, and the loan sharks certainly provided no training or insurance. Nozibeli had heard that banks lent large sums to well-off people for around two rand per hundred per month, but she knew all too well that she would never be able to take advantage of this.

The trainer also told her that she would be able, if she wanted, to come to occasional business clinics from time to time to discuss any business problems. If she fell behind in her repayments, the Start-Up Fund would be immediately informed through the electronic transfer of every movement in her account, and would request the trainer to follow up in order to see what help might be necessary.

The 300 Rand was credited to her bank account on 9 September 1995, a few days after she had filled in the form. Because she had the extra 300 Rand, Nozibeli was then able to buy 20 chickens regularly every week, instead of having to wait a week or so between purchases. She was not sure exactly what difference it had made to her income, but she reckoned that she had probably bought two more lots of chickens each month. The profit after the cost of the birds and the firewood was 115 Rand, so she had made about 230 Rand extra.

Nozibeli repaid her loan on time, at the rate of 100 Rand a month, and on 10 March 1996, six months and a day after she received her first loan, she received her second loan of 600 Rand. As with the first loan, she actually had to repay a higher amount, totalling 1,080 Rand. The same amount of 150 Rand was taken off for the GIT and 140 Rand for the SUTT, and the interest charges were naturally higher for the larger sum, but the overall cost in per centage terms was lower than for the first loan.

She used the extra money to increase her food businesses, and as winter came she was also able to buy more duvet sets. Although she had to wait three months to collect the full price of 250 Rand from her customers, she thought that the profit of 130 Rand was an excellent return on the 120 Rand she paid for each set. On 10 September 1996, a year after receiving her first loan, she received her third loan of 1,000 Rand. She would have to repay 1,440 Rand, since 200 Rand was deducted for the GIT, and a further 140 Rand for the SUTT.

Nozibeli could see from the simple schedule exactly how much she would have to repay each month, and for what purpose. If all went well, she would be eligible to receive 1,500 Rand in March 1997, and would repay 2,160 Rand, including 300 Rand for the GIT and 140 for the SUTT. In September 1997 she would be eligible for 2,000 Rand, and would have to repay 2,880, including 400 for the GUT and 140 for the SUTT. Thereafter she could continue to borrow 2,000 Rand every six months, with the same repayments, as long as she wished, although it was hoped that borrowers would then be able to 'graduate' to bank loans with lower interest rates.

The Start-Up Fund was set up in 1993 by a chartered accountant who had previously been involved in an NGO which was providing training to people like Nozibeli, and had in fact developed the Township MBA. Many of the trainees had said how they needed some capital in order to take advantage of what they had learnt, so he decided to set up the Fund in order to fill the gap.

By the end of September 1996 the Fund had advanced a total of nearly five million Rand, or over a million dollars, to about 4,800 borrowers, of whom 64 per cent were women. They were located all over South Africa, but the Start-Up Fund itself only had one office, near Cape Town. The initial client contact, the training and the follow up, or mentoring, was all provided by the twenty or so training organisations, including the founder's own previous NGO, whose services were paid for from the SUTT. The loan disbursements were all made through the bank branches, and clients' repayments through the same branches were automatically and immediately notified to the head office, so that there was no need for the Start-Up Fund itself to have any direct contact with its clients.

The Start-Up Fund, with the supporting GIT which was sufficient to cover any likely level of defaults and the SUTT which paid the full cost of training and follow up, were designed to be self-sustaining without any subsidy. The fund had received grant funds at the outset, and it was hoped that this support would continue, but the intention was to use this money to enable the Fund to accumulate substantial equity capital as quickly as possible, so that it would then be able to borrow from the commercial money markets like any other financial institution. The founder believed that external donor aid and soft loans or other local assistance would not be available for long; the development needs of South Africa were such that business development institutions would soon be required themselves to earn their living from client fees like any other businesses.

The financial position of the Fund at the end of September 1996 was as follows (amount in Rands):

Balance Sheet

Assets		Liabilities	
Loans outstanding	1,898,000	Accumulated Surplus	639,000
Fixed Assets	279,000	Loans	3,825,000
Net Current assets	2,287,000		
Total	4,464,000		4,464,000

Profit and Loss Account

Income:		
Loan interest and fees from Clients		694,000
Grants		101,000
Total		795,000
Expenditure:		
Operating Costs (including provisions)	434,000	
Interest on Loans	137,000	
Total	571,000	
Surplus		224,000

The cost of bad debts was not included in the operating costs since these were charged to the GIT, which was kept quite separate from the Start-Up Fund. During the year ending 30 September 1996 approximately 542,000 Rand, or 14 per cent of total advances, was written off and recovered from the GIT. The balance remaining in the GIT was around 300,000 Rand, three quarters of which would be distributed to clients who were fully up-to-date with their repayments, in proportion to their total repayments during the previous twelve months. This would be likely to amount to about 25 per cent of their total repayments; Nozibeli Ntuli will get around 380 Rand if she maintains her on-time repayment record.

The loans which the Start-Up Fund had borrowed for on-lending to its clients came from a variety of sources, including the Development Bank of South Africa, some trusts which major corporations had set up for social purposes, some insurance companies and so on. The interest rates varied from nil to 10 per cent per annum, and the largest loan, for some 1,900,000 Rand from the Development Bank, was at this higher rate. It was due for repayment over four years, starting in June 1997. The market rate for loans of this size between financial institutions was around 20 per cent in September 1996.

In September 1996 the South African Rand was worth approximately 25 US cents.

(Note: This case study was prepared with the help of Tony Davenport, Chief Executive of the Start-Up Fund.)

Comments and Questions

Micro-finance in South Africa is strongly influenced by two particular circumstances. Disadvantaged people in every country have increasingly to turn to self-employment for their livelihoods, but in South Africa the non-white communities are demanding and expecting dramatic economic change to match the political transformation. This places enormous pressure on enterprise development agencies and micro-finance institutions to deliver effective services.

The dual economy of South Africa, however, does confer certain advantages, which the Start-Up Fund is exploiting to the full. The banking system is as fully developed as anywhere in the world; cheques from every part of the country are cleared immediately, accounts are maintained electronically and funds transfers are immediate. This makes it possible to monitor and control a nation-wide system from one point. The Star-Up Fund delegates the handling of finance to the banks, and training, counselling and supervision to a network of local training institutions, so that it is able to service its 4,000 customers from one office. This would be impossible in most so-called 'developing countries'.

The dual society also makes it possible for modern financial institutions, such as hire purchase companies, to earn high profits from unsophisticated customers. This may benefit both parties, but it can also lead to exploitation. It is impossible to calculate exactly what interest rate the Star-Up Fund's customers are paying, because training and counselling are included in the package as well as loans, and borrowers are also eligible to receive a share of the balance remaining in the guarantee fund at the end of each period, but it is certainly not cheap money.

Questions

1) Ms. Nozibeli had to pay a total of 700 Rand, over six months, in order to get her first 300 Rand loan. She paid 1,080 Rand for the second six-month loan of 600 Rand, and the corresponding figures for the following three loans, all for six months, were: 1,440 Rand for 1,000 Rand, 2,160 Rand for 1,500 Rand and 2,880 for 2,000 Rand. These payments included the cost of training, and counselling and supervision, and the net cost would be reduced when she received her refund from the guarantee fund. She herself calculated that the total cost was lower than she would have paid a 'loan shark' for the loan without any other services. Are the payments excessive, should the non-financial services be 'bundled' with the loan, or should clients be allowed to take a loan without other services if they wish ?

2) Banking services are being modernised and improved very rapidly in many countries. How can micro-finance institutions in less-developed countries use modern banking services to improve their services to their clients ?

3) The financial results of the Start-Up Fund suggest that it can be very profitable. Does this not demonstrate that micro-finance systems, when properly designed and managed, can be good investments in themselves, so that grants and subsidised loans are no longer necessary and may actually be delaying the growth of the industry ?

CHAPTER 18

THE KALANJIAM COMMUNITY BANKING SYSTEM, MADURAI EAST, TAMIL NADU, INDIA

Madurai East is one of the poorer parts of the State of Tamil Nadu in southern India. The economy is based on agriculture, and much of the land is served by a canal irrigation system, but the land holdings are small, and the majority of the 100,000 villagers in the area are marginal farmers, share croppers and agricultural labourers, for whom employment is available only for part of the year. When the people need finance, for production or consumption, they borrow money from moneylenders at high interest rates. One common method is the paddy interest system; loans are given in cash at the beginning of the agricultural season and at the end of the season the principal is repaid in cash and interest is paid in the form of two to three bags of paddy per Rs. 1,000 borrowed; one bag of paddy is worth around three hundred rupees.

PRADAN, or Professional Assistance for Development Action, is an Indian NGO which was started by a group of management professionals from India's top management schools. PRADAN's staff have always tried to facilitate the development of autonomous people's institutions in the communities where they work, rather than perpetuating their own role, and their work in financial services has been consistent with this philosophy. PRADAN have livelihood programmes in many different parts of India, and Madurai is one of their main centres of activity.

When they came to Madurai East the PRADAN staff found that the people were using a system of contract labour groups known as *Kothu*. They undertook farm work for landowners on a collective basis, in order to maximise their individual earnings. This tradition of group working helped PRADAN to initiate a group-based women's banking programme in Madurai East in 1990. The primary objective was to provide access and control over credit to poor women at the level of the smallest and most disadvantaged village communities or hamlets. This was achieved through the creation of hamlet level groups of around fifteen or twenty women with regular savings and credit activities. The groups were called kalanjiams, which is a Tamil word for a grain storage jar.

In order to ensure that these groups would be sustainable and could link with formal financial institutions, PRADAN evolved a three-tier system; about fifteen kalanjiams join together to form a cluster Nidhi, or fund, and there is also a federation which is made up of around two hundred kalanjiams. The Vaigai Vattara Kalanjiam (VVK) Federation is the longest established of these federations. It was started in 1995 and covers the whole of Madurai East. By the end of March 1997 the VVK had 202 member kalanjiams, and was itself taking over the group formation and training process from PRADAN. The aim was to achieve a total membership of 400 kalanjiam groups, with some 6,000 members, by 1998.

Mathur colony is a small hamlet of about forty houses about 20 km from Madurai, the old temple city which is the administrative headquarters of Madurai District, of which Madurai East is a part. The hamlet lies between paddy fields and irrigation tanks, in a broad valley surrounded by rocky hills. It appears prosperous, with green paddy fields and groves of palm and coconut trees here and there, but the majority of the inhabitants of the hamlet are agricultural labourers with no land of their own. They do some share cropping from time to time, using the land of their better-off neighbours from the main village of Mathur which is about one kilometre away. Most of the children of the colony go to school, but none of the women is literate. A few of the men have attended primary school and can read and write.

A PRADAN fieldworker initiated a kalanjiam group of 25 women in Mathur Colony in December 1990. The leader had been a member of a Kothu labour group, and she therefore had some experience of organisation. The members agreed to save Rs.10 a month each, and after six months PRADAN matched their savings of Rs. 1,500 with a grant of the same amount. PRADAN discontinued these grants after a year, since they were found to raise unrealistic expectations. The group members started to borrow small sums of Rs. 100 to 300 from their accumulated savings and the PRADAN grant, and all went well for another five months. Then one member who had taken a larger than usual loan of Rs. 1,000 from the group started to be irregular in her repayments. When she was pressed to pay she created problems in the group, and they eventually decided to split.

PRADAN asked the members of the kalanjiam to hand over the common fund they had accumulated from interest payments on their loans, together with the matching grant from PRADAN, to another group in a nearby community, but five of the members decided that they would not allow the kalanjiam to dissolve and would run it at any cost. They continued their operations with the PRADAN grant and their share of the savings. After three months another nine members joined. Since that time the kalanjiam has had 14 members.

The members increased their monthly savings contribution to Rs. 30 per month in addition to savings in various kalanjiam chits or savings funds. When the Shri Meenakshiamman Cluster Nidhi was formed in late 1993 they became active members, and they borrowed money from the Nidhi to help meet the members' increasing needs for finance. This was not, however, sufficient to meet their needs, and the members were therefore looking out for other sources of funds. In 1995 their adviser from PRADAN suggested that one option might be to try to take a loan from a commercial bank under the self-help group linkage programme which had been introduced in 1990, but was only very slowly being taken up by the banks in the field.

The Mathur Colony kalanjiam had an account with the Appantirupati branch of Indian Overseas Bank (IOB), and were used to dealing with this bank. IOB is one of the large government owned national commercial banks. In an attempt to bring financial services to the whole population, the government had divided the whole of rural India into what were called 'service areas'. Each such area was allocated to one branch of a commercial bank, which was then responsible for delivering the quota of subsidised credit schemes to that area. Inevitably, this discouraged competition, and if people did not get what they wanted from the branch which covered their service area it was difficult to persuade another bank to work with them.

Mathur Colony is part of the service area of the Appantirupati branch of Indian Overseas Bank, and the kalanjiam members submitted an application for a loan under the linkage programme to this branch. The manager, however, was not interested in lending to them. There were several people who had defaulted on government sponsored loan schemes in the surrounding area, and he was not interested in lending through groups when some of the members' husbands might have overdue loans. The members totally failed in their efforts to persuade him to lend them money.

In February 1996, however, the manager of the Mangulam branch of Canara Bank, another of the national commercial banks which had taken up the self-help linkage programme with some enthusiasm and worked in close collaboration with PRADAN, said they would be interested in working with some of the kalanjiam groups which PRADAN had promoted. He was willing to accept customers from beyond the service area of his own branch, and five of the strongest of the eleven groups in the Mathur cluster, including the Mathur colony kalanjiam, were chosen to receive loans.

The group members, together with their Cluster Associate, the Nidhi Manager and the PRADAN fieldworker, discussed how they should use the loan. They decided that the money would be lent to three or four only of the 14 members, so that they could each have a reasonable sum and put it to a genuinely productive use instead of dividing the money into a larger number of small loans which would yield little benefit. The bank manager stipulated that any members whose husbands were in arrears with the other bank should not borrow from their loan. The group agreed that this was reasonable from the bank's point of view. They realised that it was not right for people to have the impression that they could borrow from one bank, not repay, and then get a loan from another neighbouring bank.

In February 1996 the Mathur Colony kalanjiam submitted an application for Rs. 21,000 to Canara Bank, to be borrowed at the fixed interest rate for self help groups of 12 per cent per year. They agreed that the loan was to be lent at 2 per cent per month, or 24 per cent per year, to these members for the following purposes:

To Panchu - Rs. 7,000 to lease some land for farming.
To Manthaiammal - Rs. 7,000 also for leasing land.
To Santhi - Rs. 7,000 to repay a 10 per cent a month loan to a moneylender.

The group leaders then went to the bank three or four times but each time the manager said he was too busy and asked them to come after some time. In spite of their disappointment, they patiently went again and again.

In the meantime, Santhi's debt had to be repaid as the moneylender was putting a lot of pressure on her and the interest was mounting rapidly. Manthaiammal also urgently needed her money for the land lease since if she failed to take the lease in April the land would not be available again for the whole year. The group had to find another source of money for their members, so they took a loan of Rs. 14,000 from their Cluster Nidhi to tide them over. This was enough to repay Santhi's debt and for Manthaiammal's land lease; Panchu managed to persuade the landowner to let her start cultivating the land but to wait some time for the money.

The Nidhi loan was only a temporary expedient, however, and the group still needed to borrow from the Bank. PRADAN organised two special training programmes for the leaders of the groups which were going to borrow from the bank, and eventually the loans were sanctioned. When the group leaders went to the bank, the manager said that the loan should not be used for clearing old debts since this would not produce extra income for the borrower to use for repayment. The leaders convinced the manager that this would not happen in their case; they said they were willing to give their personal guarantees for the loan, in addition to the guarantee from the kalanjiam. The kalanjiam members then had to decide to whom this loan should be given as the earlier plan had been partially completed with money from the Cluster Nidhi.

Panchu took Rs. 9,000 for the land lease as was earlier decided. She had been one of the first members to join the kalanjiam when it was formed, and was initially elected as the treasurer. Later, when the Cluster Nidhi was formed, she took on responsibilities at this level too.

Panchu used her Rs. 9,000 to lease half an acre of single crop land for three years for paddy cultivation. The landowner agreed to return the Rs. 9,000 to her on completion of the three years, and she also had the option of extending the lease for another two to three years. The interest rate charged by the kalanjiam is 2 per cent per month. Eight months after she had taken the loan, Panchu had paid Rs. 1,400 of the principal and Rs. 1,328 towards interest.

During 1996 Panchu harvested 12 bags of paddy of which two were distributed as wages. The value of the remaining ten bags was Rs. 3,200, at the going rate of Rs. 320 per bag. She also got Rs. 500 worth of paddy straw, so the total return from the land for the year was Rs. 3,700. She spent Rs. 1,000 on fertilisers and ploughing. Panchu and her family provided most of the labour.

This extra income has enabled Panchu to meet her household expenses and to pay for part of the food requirements of her family. She no longer has to look for labouring work, since she can work on the land she has leased, and if she had taken the loan from a moneylender she would have had to pay the higher interest rate of about five per cent per month.

The second borrower was Arnavalli, who was lent Rs. 9,000 to repay an old debt. Arnavalli and her husband live in Mathur Colony. Their two sons aged nine and six are going to school. She was one of the two first members who started the kalanjiam in Mathur Colony in December 1990. In the early days of the group she borrowed Rs. 7,000 to repay an old debt under the paddy interest system. This loan had been taken by her husband at the time of their marriage 10 years back and for more than five years had been paying the paddy interest alone. Her first kalanjiam loan enabled them at last to clear this debt, and this increased her faith in the kalanjiam and made her a more active member.

In June 1996 Arnavalli had begun to face a lot of pressure from a moneylender from whom she taken a loan some time earlier at 10 per cent interest per month. She had been unable to pay even the interest for some time. The family owned two bullocks and one milch animal which were their main source of income apart from what they could earn from agricultural labour. She was under such pressure that she felt that the only thing she could do was to sell the animals to repay the debt and accumulated interest. She had virtually decided to take this drastic step, and was about to do it.

The kalanjiam members heard about her plight and decided that it was the duty of the kalanjiam to help her. They felt that it would be a serious and perhaps permanent blow to the family if she sold the assets which were their main source of income. The loan from Canara Bank was disbursed at about the same time, and although the group had decided not to encourage too many loans for settling old debts they decided to give a loan to Arnavalli in view of her circumstances.

After a lot of discussion the group members decided to lend her Rs. 9,000. She repaid Rs. 7,000 of the interest and principal she owed on her 10 per cent monthly interest loan, and she used Rs. 2,000 to repay the principal of another short-term paddy loan. This helped settle her most immediate and pressing debtors. She still owed Rs. 3,000 on another 10 per cent interest loan and two other jewel loans for which she has pawned 8 grams of gold; she plans to clear these loans in due course.

In order to help her resist any pressure to sell the animals to clear these loans, and to ensure that the Kalanjiam loan really achieved its purpose, the group asked Arnavalli to promise that she would not sell her animals before she had repaid the full amount to the Kalanjiam. Arnavalli was delighted that she has saved her productive assets from being sold, and the Kalanjiam members were all pleased to have been able to help their fellow-member in the time of her need.

The third borrower was Pandiamma. The group decided to lend her Rs. 3,000 to repay old debts. She had borrowed small amounts from different people some years back, and she had only been able to pay the interest and a very small amount towards the principal. She used the Rs. 3,000 she had borrowed from the Kalanjiam to repay the principal and interest on four small loans.

The bank had fixed a repayment period of three years, but the leaders told the members that they should try to repay in a shorter period. They also decided that the members should repay principal and interest every month to the Kalanjiam, and that the Kalanjiam should repay the Bank in the same way. They could have decided to repay quarterly or half yearly, or even to keep the money revolving among themselves until the date when it was due to be repaid to the bank, but they were anxious if possible to repay before the scheduled date. They felt that this would make their first loan a good experience for the bank and for the Kalanjiam, and they knew that they could always take a second loan once the first one was repaid.

The Manager of the Canara Bank branch especially praised the Mathur Colony Kalanjiam for their regular repayments and for keeping their word. The members were very proud of this.

By the end of January 1997 the group were paying the cost of their own management, their part-time group accountant, and their share of the management costs of the Cluster Nidhi.

The financial position of the Mathur Colony Kalanjiam was approximately as follows (in Indian rupees):

Balance Sheet

Assets	31 Mar 1996	31 Jan 1997
Loans with members	74,400	97,000
Deposit with Nidhi	3,700	4,700
Cash in hand	1,600	2,800
Cash in Bank	2,600	700
Total	82,300	105,200
Liabilities		
Reserves & Surplus	7,900	12,700
Savings	20,200	21,000
Loans & Advances	53,000	70,000
Provision for overdues	1,200	1,200
Risk fund	–	300
Total	82,300	105,200

Profit and Loss Statement

	1 Apr 95 - 31 Mar 96	1 Apr 96 - 31 Jan 97
Income		
Interest earned on loans	Rs 13,800	Rs 17,600
Service cost	1,400	200
Total	Rs 15,200	Rs 17,800
Expenditure		
Interest paid on loans/savings	Rs 7,400	Rs 9,200
Service cost to Nidhi	600	600
Training & Meeting expenses	1,500	1,300
Printing & Stationary	400	300
Group accountant salary	600	1,000
Misc. Expenses	1,400	600
Profit	3,300	4,800
Total	Rs 15,200	Rs 17,800

Meenakshiamman Nidhi—Mathur Cluster Association

The Mathur Colony Kalanjiam is part of the Mathur Cluster Association. Six months after the first groups had been started the leaders from the different groups started to meet one another and share their experience. They discussed various issues related to savings and lending and the management of the groups. At first these meetings were informal and irregular.

As the savings of the groups increased, and their funds were further augmented by the PRADAN matching grants, they were able to increase the amounts they lent to their members. After about a year some of the groups became less committed. Some members' repayments became irregular and their fellow members ceased to be concerned, and some other groups became dominated by self-interested leaders and the members lost their feeling of ownership. There were also some changes among the PRADAN staff which reduced their contact with groups for a period. A few groups became totally defunct, and only six remained in operation.

At one of their informal cluster meetings some of the groups decided that they should themselves take some initiative, rather than relying on PRADAN always to solve all their problems. They chose a few of the more capable leaders to form part of the Cluster Association which would support and strengthen the groups, with the help of two or three representatives from each group. With the support of the PRADAN fieldworker these leaders helped the six groups which remained to return to regular functioning.

Their members agreed that they wanted to take bigger loans in order to improve their income, and the fieldworker said that PRADAN would be willing to provide some support for them if they could put together a reasonable request for funds. The cluster committee asked each group to bring together the requirements of its members; they then consolidated the demands from the different groups and presented a proposal to PRADAN for Rs. 54,000, which was duly approved.

This was a turning point where the people's need and PRADAN's aim of improving livelihoods matched. There was some confusion as to the financial role of the new Cluster Association. Finally after a lot of discussions it was decided that finance and the promotional and support functions were fundamentally different and should be handled separately. Hence on July 3rd 1993 they established the Cluster Meenakshiamman Cluster Nidhi, or fund, which was to manage the financial functions. Its purpose was to act as a financial intermediary between other financial institutions and the Kalanjian groups. The Cluster Association also has separate working groups made up of elected representations from the member Kalanjians. These deal with other promotion functions such as training, the development of new groups, general community issues and monitoring and evaluation.

One Director from each group was elected to the Nidhi Board of Directors, and each Kalanjiam group subscribed Rs. 1,000 Share capital to the Nidhi. The Board of Directors then framed its bye-laws. The Kalanjiam groups would be members of the Nidhi and not the individual members, and the Nidhi would tend to the groups which would in turn lend to their members. The groups would be free to charge whatever rate of interest they wished to their members on money which was borrowed from the Nidhi. This was the first Nidhi; by March 1997 there were 19 such Nidhis in operation in different locations around Madurai.

The financial position of the Sri Meenakshiamman Nidhi was approximately as follows (in Indian rupees):

Balance Sheet

Assets	31 Mar 1996	31 Jan 1997
Loans to members	228,500	383,200
Advances	4,500	2,000
Cash in hand	200	2,200
Cash at bank	56,200	3,900
Stocks of stationary for sale to groups	17,900	—
Total	307,300	391,300
Liabilities		
General reserve	48,600	39,500
Savings	15,700	29,300
Deposits from groups	12,000	18,600
Loan from VVK Federation	—	70,700
Risk fund	1,500	3,700
Revolving fund from Pradan	229,500	229,500
Total	307,300	391,300

Profit and Loss Statement for the Period

	1 Apr 95–31 Mar 96	1 Apr. 96–31 Jan 97
Income		
Support cost from Pradan	16,000	—
Interest earned	35,800	26,700
Service cost	5,600	5,100
Risk fund	—	5,000
Other income	3,400	5,000
Total	60,800	36,800
Expenditure		
Manager & Associate salary	12,400	11,300
Interest paid	600	1,200
Rent	2,400	2,400
Training & meeting expenses	5,500	4,300
Admin. Expenses	5,500	5,300
Misc. expnses	5,400	—
Stationery	1,000	100
Audit fee	—	500
Excess of income over Expenditure	28,000	11,700
Total	60,800	36,800

Vaigai Vattara Kalanjiam—An Autonomous Federation of Kalanjians

The Mathur colony Kalanjiam and the Meenakshiamman Nidhi do not function in isolation. In 1995, towards the end of the fifth year of the community credit operation, the need for a central third level institution, or Federation, began to be felt. There were a number of formal and informal meetings at the level of the kalanjiams and the Clusters, and the form of the federation slowly emerged and began to take shape.

In early 1996 the Federation was registered as the Vaigai Vattara Kalanjiam and began its functions formally. One of the main reasons for its establishment was the realisation that although 29 kalanjiams had borrowed directly from Canara Bank under the self-help group linkage scheme, the financial needs of their members would soon outstrip the direct borrowing capacity of the kalanjiams. As their livelihood activities expanded they would need more finance than they could get through their kalanjiams.

There were a number of institutions which were willing to provide finance for such people, but they wanted to deal with a more substantial intermediary than a Kalanjiam or a cluster Nidhi. Canara Bank itself lent Rs. 300,000 to the Vaigai Vattara Kalanjiam, and the Small industries Development Bank of India (SIDBI) lent another Rs. 400,000 which would not have been accessible to the kalanjiams in any other way.

The Federation is registered as a Society, and is managed by a Board of Directors who form its Executive Committee. One Director is elected from every ten to fifteen kalanjiams in a geographical area to represent them on the Board. The Federation has a Managing Director and an Accountant, and it is planned to have seven Cluster Associates and four Cluster Nidhi managers on the full-time staff before the end of 1997. All these staff members will be locally recruited, and all but one have been working with the clusters as group accountants and cluster associates. Basically, the federation is taking over and developing many of the roles which were previously performed by PRADAN.

The Cluster Associates look after the overall development of the kalanjiams, they do internal auditing for the groups and they act as financial counsellors for the members. The work with the active support of the Cluster Committees who are representatives of groups at Cluster level. The Cluster Managers take care of the Nidhis with the support of their boards, and help to ensure that the loans given by the Nidhis to the kalanjiams are properly used and recovered.

The Federation's activities are coordinated by areas level 'Cluster committees' of five to six members from the kalanjiams in a given cluster, and all the Kalanjiam representatives in a cluster meet once a month to discuss the activities of the kalanjiams and processing of new loans. Each committee has a set of guidelines for the proper functioning of their cluster and its member kalanjiams.

The Federation provides bulk finance to the cluster Nidhis to finance the kalanjiams when their own resources are not enough to meet the needs of the individual members. The main use of the loans which the kalanjiams take from the Federation is for income generation. The money is also used for paying off old debts and for housing.

The cluster Nidhis pay 12 per cent annual interest to the Federation and they lend to the Kalanjians at between 15 and 18 per cent. This is of course higher than the 12 per cent which the Kalanjians have to pay to the Banks, but in most cases the Kalanjians prefer to borrow from the Nidhi, in spite of the higher interest rate, because the service is quicker and more flexible. Most banks do not yet perceive loans to kalanjians as potential business, and the Mangulam branch of Canara bank, from which the Mathur Colony Kalanjian took a loan, is exceptional. It is hoped that the banks will eventually offer the same level of service as the Nidhi so that the Nidhi's role will be to facilitate links between the banks and its member Kalanjians rather than acting as a lender itself.

The Kalanjians on-lend to their members at between two and three per cent a month, or 24 per cent to 36 per cent annually. Kalanjians in the first year of so of existence often charge up to 5 per cent a month for small loans which members take for medical expenses, festivals and so on. As the groups mature and start giving larger loans for investment purposes they usually reduce the interest on all the loans, but some maintain the higher rates for small consumption loans. The decision is of course entirely theirs.

In addition to providing credit, the Federation plays the same development role which PRADAN performed when it initiated the programme in 1990. Its staff, with the voluntary assistance of members, helps to promote new Kalanjians and to support existing ones, and offers an increasing range of other services. These include a simple life insurance plan. Each member of such groups as wish to joint pays Rs. 50 a year, and his family is eligible to receive Rs. 10,000 on the member's death. This is presently done through an insurance company, but when sufficient members subscribe it should be a viable product for the Federation itself to offer. Livestock insurance is also available from the Federation, and is mainly used by members of the women's dairy business association which PRADAN has promoted as part of its non-financial livelihood promotion activity.

The Federation also helps the kalanjiam members in their continuing struggle for social justice. In early 1997, for instance, a member's husband was killed in an industrial accident. His employers offered the member an ex-gratia payment of Rs. 70,000, but her husband's parents, supported by influential people in their village, demanded that the money should be given to them rather than to the widow and her children. The VVK organised a massive protest and PRADAN's staff also supported the women; it appeared that there intervention would swing the case in her favour.

The VVK Federation held its Annual General meeting on their new plot of land on Sunday 20 April 1997. This was the same day as an important religious festival, and the Federation's plot is on the main road along which the image of a local deity is carried in processing on that day.

It was normal for wealthy landowners and businessmen to construct lavish pavilions along the roadside on this occasion, and for the procession to halt for them to pay their respects to the deity. The temple authorities expected a donation of around Rs. 20,000 for this service, but the Federation was able to persuade them to accept a reduced payment of Rs. 2,000 to allow their members to enjoy the same privilege. This was a major social innovation, since the honour was usually extended only to upper caste wealthy men; the Federation's members were lower caste, poor and female.

About 2,500 members attended the meeting. They paraded to the site in separate groups for each cluster, holding banners and preceded by dancers and by groups of women playing trumpets. The members of each group carried heavy jars of paddy on their heads. These were poured into enormous kalanjiam pots, as an offering to the god but also as a contribution to the Federation's funds; the total worth of the grain which was donated was about Rs. 3,000. The full pots were crowned with sweet smelling coconut blossoms, and the rice overflowed into great heaps beside them.

After numerous speeches and songs about the need for solidarity and regular saving and repayment, the accountant read out the balance sheet and profit and loss account for the year ended 31 March 1997. The figures were approximately as follow (in Indian Rupees):

Assets		Liabilities	
Cash	7,500	Various advances	9,100
Bank balance	189,400	Chit funds	5,600
Loans of members	614,100	Life insurance	25,500
Advance rent	4,400	Livestock insurance	19,700
Stocks	2,700	SIDBI Loan	400,000
Land	143,000	Canara Bank loan	300,000
		Risk fund	4,700
		Vehicle fund	107,600
		Retained profit	42,200
		Members shared	46,700
Total	961,100	Total	961,100

The land was bought during the year for construction of a Federation headquarters; the construction cost was likely to be around Rs. 500,000, and would be met with a capital grant from SIDBI and a special collection by members of Rs. 100,000.

The loans from SIDBI and Canara Bank were only received towards the end of the financial year; hence these accounts give a low figure for bank interest received. The proceeds of these loans had not been disbursed to groups at the time of these accounts.

The grant from SIDBI is a one-off component of its bulk lending programme to NGOs such as PRADAN, and will not be repeated. The grant and donations from PRADAN and other sources, and the reimbursement of the training costs, will continue on a declining basis.

The approximate operating figures for the year ending 31 March 1997 were as follows:

Profit and Loss Account

Income:		
Interest on Loans		17,800
Interest on bank deposit		600
Training costs refunded		20,000
Grant from PRADAN		68,900
Grants from SIDBI		50,000
Member subscriptions		3000
Donations		68,000
Total		228,300
Expenses:		
Interest paid	18,300	
Administration	166,400	
Total	184,700	
Profit		43,600

The vehicle fund is made up of the profit that has been accumulated by the Federation over three years from operating a small bus. This bus belongs to PRADAN but the Federation has been running it as a business operation for three years; they are allowed to keep the profits they earn after paying for fuel, maintenance and wages, and they do not pay any rent to PRADAN for the bus itself.

The meeting was attended by representatives of PRADAN and by bankers and other local dignitaries. It was however organised, directed and paid for by the members themselves, and the visitors were there as guests rather than as supervisors or sponsors. It was clear that the Federation, and its constituent cluster Nidhis and kalanjiams, were confident and autonomous local organisations with which PRADAN, the banks and others could in future work as equal partners in the process of community development.

(Note: The material for this case study was contributed by Ms. Raghini of Pradhan Madurai.)

(The rate of exchange is approximately Rs. 35 = $ 1.00.)

Comments and Questions

The Madurai Kalanjians, and their Cluster Nidhis and Federation, are an excellent example of the multi-tier people's financial institutions that are being promoted from number of NGOs in India. They differ very significantly from the other institutions so far described, since they are promoted but clearly not owned by the NGO, and they are very much member-controlled. The Urban Cooperative bank in Cuttack is nominally member-owned, but like most large cooperative institutions it is managed in a similar way to a shareholder owned company. The Kalanjians were started by their members, the clusters were started by the Kalanjians and the Federation itself was also initiated by the members.

This type of organisation is of course similar to the original concept of cooperatives, with secondary unions and third level apex organisations. The Madurai groups are not associated with official Cooperative system, because it has been so politicised and corrupted, but the members are in a sense going back to the original Raiffeisen approach to rural finance which was started in Germany in the nineteenth century.

The Kalanjians have avoided the ills of the official cooperatives but they will still be vulnerable to the problems that affect all forms of group-owned enterprise, particularly when PRADAN has completely withdrawn. They may be 'hijacked' by a minority of the members, they may not be willing or able to afford the best professional management, and the delays and other weaknesses which are inevitably associated with group decision-making may make it difficult to compete as rural financial markets become more competitive.

Madurai has a very bad record for female infanticide and gender discrimination in general. This make social empowerment all the more important for the women, and the high visibility of the Federation's annual meeting clearly contributes very powerfully to this. The current operating figures suggest that this function is being performed both profitably and effectively.

Questions

1) Rural people need equitable and efficient financial services, and they need them urgently. Would it not be quicker and more efficient for Pradan actually to own and manage the Federation, if not the Cluster Nidhis, to service the needs of the Kalanjians ?

2) Some banks are willing to deal direct with the Kalanjian self-help groups, and more banks should enter this market in the future. Should the Clusters and the Federation plan in the medium- to long-term to withdraw from any direct role in financial intermediation, and confine themselves to training, facilitation and advocacy, leaving the field clear for the banks ?

3) Alternatively, it may be that the banks will never become serious contenders in the field of micro-finance. Should organisations such as the Kalanjian community banking system work to create wholly new financial structures, through links with other similar groups elsewhere, so

that they can eventually compete in national and even international financial markets, by-passing the existing banks altogether ?

4) The meetings of the Kalanjians, the Clusters and the Federation combine business with religion, and even the detailed procedure of the Federation meeting is very similar in many ways to the ritual of local religious festivals. Is this combination likely to strengthen or weaken the commercial viability of the new financial system, in the long term ?

CHAPTER 19

BASIX FINANCE, RAICHUR, KARNATAKA, INDIA

The Bangle Trader

Sakuntia is a member of a traditional entertainers caste; she lives in Boidoddi, a small village in Karnataka State of India, near to the border of Andhra Pradesh. Her husband owns one-and-a-half acres of land, but apart from cultivating this he has no work; they have eight children, and the family depends mainly on what Sakuntia herself can earn. Her caste used to earn a living from dancing and singing, but nowadays she and many others sell bangles, plastic toys and other simple gift items at village markets and festivals. She buys about Rs. 2,000 worth of stock at one time from wholesalers in Raichur, the market town 10 km away, or from Hyderabad. She can usually sell this amount in one month, and since she normally sells her goods for double what they cost her she earns about Rs. 2,000 a month. She has to pay about a hundred rupees a month for transport, but this is still much more remunerative, and less laborious, than working in the village brick factory for around Rs. 40 a day.

Sakuntia had heard about various government loan schemes, but nobody in her community had every benefited from them. Like everyone else who did any business, she used to borrow working capital from the local moneylenders. They charged 3 per cent interest a month, and they did not take any security; they lived in the same village and knew whom they could trust. She used to have to go round to two or three lenders to get the money, because no single person was willing to advance her the full Rs. 2,000 that she needed. This took up a lot of her valued time, and she always disliked having to beg for money from her neighbours.

Sakuntia was therefore very happy when she heard in June 1996 that a new financial institution called Basix had been set up in Raichur, and that it was willing to lend money to self-help groups of women who could then borrow from their group fund to finance their own activities. She suggested to five of her friends who were in the same business that they should get together and form a group so that they could borrow from Basix. They started their group, which they called the Dasaru Sangha, in

October 1996, with Rs. 200 each. They first had to deposit with Basix, one-eighth of the sum they wished to borrow, and by April 1997 they had borrowed and repaid four loans.

Their fifth loan was for a total of Rs. 12,000 or Rs. 2,000 each. The money-lenders used to demand that their loans should be repaid in one lump sum, at the end of the month, but the Basix representative visited Boidoddi village regularly, and the members could also repay their loans at the Basix branch in the market yard in Raichur. Basix was willing to accept repayments at any time, so that the members, and the group, only had to pay interest when they actually needed the money.

Basix charges 21 per cent interest, and the women themselves pay 24 per cent interest, or 2 per cent a month, to their group. Basix pays them 12 per cent annual interest on their Rs. 1,500 deposit, and they hope that their own fund will grow so that they will eventually not need to borrow any more. Sakuntia and her five friends are happy with the new arrangement; it is quicker and easier to borrow money and to repay, they pay less interest, and they also feel that there new group gives them more status in the community. Several other women in the village are planning to follow the example and to form groups so that they too can borrow from Basix.

The Potters' Colony

There is a small potters' colony of eleven families in the village of Singanodi, near to Raichur. The women hand mould-clay *chulas*, or traditional stoves, and it takes about one hour to make one stove. The women usually make about four *chulas* a day, since they need the rest of the time for their domestic work, and to take care of their goats and small kitchen gardens. They have to hire bullock carts to fetch clay and firewood, and they also have to pay the owners of the land where they dig the clay. The cost of the materials and transport is about Rs. 10 per stove. In addition, they have to pay about Rs. 3 per stove for transport to Raichur.

The potters have always been very poor, and until recently they had to borrow money from a merchant in Raichur to pay for these inputs. The only way he would accept repayment was in the form of the finished stoves; he would pay them Rs. 28 for each stove, but would deduct Rs. 13 to repay his loan, leaving the women with only Rs. 15 for all their hard work. The women knew that people in their own village would pay a higher price, but they were 'tied' to the man who lent them the working capital.

In mid-1996 the women of Singanodi heard that Basix was willing to lend money to people such as themselves. Six of the women, together with three men, formed a group which they called the Kumbara Sangha. They agreed that Rs. 200 each was the minimum sum they needed in order to free at least some of their production from dependence on the merchant. The Basix representative told them that they would have to deposit one-eighth of whatever they wished to borrow, and by August they had managed to save Rs. 25 each. They then deposited the total of Rs. 225 with Basix, and a few days later they received their first loan of Rs. 1,800.

When they had completed their next load of stoves the women found that they could sell them in the village for as much as Rs. 40; after deducting the cost of the inputs, this left them with Rs. 30, which was twice as much as they had earned before.

There was a high demand for the stoves, from the village people and merchants, and the members of the Kumbara Sangha repaid their loan in three months. In October they borrowed Rs. 3,600 and in early December they took Rs. 9,000. This was the best selling season, and the group were able to repay this third loan and to borrow a further Rs. 15,000 before the end of the month. They cleared this in April 1997, and then applied to borrow Rs. 20,000. By that time, they had saved enough to make the necessary deposit of one-eighth of the loan, or Rs. 2,500, without difficulty.

Sunflower and Paddy Growing, Linked via a Large Processing Company

Ms. Kuppamma and her husband farm eight acres of irrigated land and two acres of dry land near the village of Gillesugur in Raichur District of Karnataka. Their main crops are sunflower and paddy. Until mid-1996 they used to sell their sunflower crop through a commission agent in Raichur market yard. They used to finance the crop with a loan from the agent, at 3 per cent interest a month, and this meant that they had to sell the crop through the same agent; the price was determined by the market, but Ms. Kuppamma was never sure that her crop was weighed correctly.

Ms. Kuppamma had heard that ITC Agrotech, a subsidiary of one of India's largest companies, paid higher prices for sunflower seed. This company owned the largest oil mill in India, which was quite closed to her village, and it was running at well below capacity because of a shortage of sunflower seed. ITC, however, did not have any scheme for financing the growers, so that small farmers like Ms. Kuppamma had to sell through commission agents who were willing to advance them money at the beginning of the season.

In June 1996 the ITC Agrotech field representative told Ms. Kuppamma that his company had recently made and experimental arrangement with a new financial institution called Basix which had just started operations in Raichur market yard. ITC had lent a large sum of money to Basix, which they in turn were lending to selected small growers such as Ms. Kuppamma to finance their sunflower crop, on the condition that it would be sole to ITC. The interest rate was 2 per cent a month, and the growers had to agree to allow ITC to repay Basix from the sales proceeds of their crops.

Ms. Kuppamma happily agreed to participate. The Basix representative who visited her said that she would have to be a member of a group of five, each of whom would agree to guarantee the others' loans. She persuaded four other farmers to join her, and she then borrowed Rs. 9,000 from Basix in July 1996. This loan was disbursed in kind, for seed, fertiliser and pesticides. She sold her complete crop to ITC for Rs. 39,000 when it was harvested in December. She was able to repay the whole amount, plus interest, when the crop was harvested in December, and ITC repaid the Rs. 9,000 loan to Basix on her behalf, plus interest of Rs. 1,080.

She estimated that she had benefited in three ways. First, ITC had paid about Rs. 100 a quintal more than the current price at the market yard, and this increase was worth about Rs. 3,000. Secondly, the lower interest rate had saved her Rs. 540, and thirdly, ITC had covered the cost of transporting the sunflower from her farm to its factory. Also, she was sure that the crop had been correctly weighed, and ITC had supplied good quality inputs, at a fair price, as well as providing advice which helped her to grow a better and higher-value crop.

Ms. Kuppamma soon found that there were other benefits to be gained from her first successful season. Her next crop was paddy, for which she would previously have borrowed Rs. 12,000 from moneylenders at 3 per cent interest a month. Paddy could be sold to any rice mill, or even in the village itself, so the lender had no protection, but the Basix representative told her that as a good client she could now borrow direct from Basix; the interest rate was 2 per cent a month, and this alone would mean a saving of Rs. 720 on her six-month loan. Ms. Kuppamma and two other members of her group took loans on this basis.

With the paddy harvested and sold, and the Basix land repaid, Ms. Kuppamma wants to take a composite loan for the whole of the following year. She will still grow sunflower and paddy, and the sunflower loan will be repaid through ITC, but there will be only one loan agreement, for two disbursements and two repayments. Formerly, Ms. Kuppamma had to spend a day or two for each crop, going round from one moneylender to another to get the amount she required. Now she will be able to arrange her finances for the whole year in one simple transaction.

Borrowing through the Market Yard

Ms. Hanumakka grows paddy on her farm and sells it through a commission agent in Raichur market. She has always faced difficulty in obtaining the Rs. 3,000 she needed to finance her crop. Sometimes she could get an advance from a commission agent for a few hundred rupees at about 3 per cent interest a month, and she would have to borrow the balance from a local moneylender at about 5 per cent. It always took a long time to secure the money, and she sometimes had to pay fees to intermediaries for them to speak to the moneylenders on her behalf.

In mid-1996 she contacted a new commission agent, Mr. Mallikarjun, of Birlingeshwara Traders, in order to see if he would be willing to advance her some money. He was trying to establish his company's position as a buyer, and one way of doing this was to advance loans to farmers, so that they would sell their crops to him. The banks were willing to lend money to finance stocks, but not for on-lending to farmers, so he had to look elsewhere for funds for this purpose. He borrowed some money from his relatives who were commission agents in the nearby cotton market, but this was not enough. He then came into contact with Basix, the new financial institution which had recently started operations from a branch office in the market yard near to his office. This was in itself unusual, since most bankers did not think the market yard was a suitable place to locate a branch.

Ms. Hanumakka found that Mr. Mallikarjun had borrowed Rs 300,000 from Basix, specifically for on-lending to farmers such as herself. He had about 800 customers, but he had decided to lend the money to 100 select suppliers in two villages, in order to secure their loyalty. He had no fear about non-payment, since he knew the villages quite well and the village people all knew that even if one of their number defaulted, none of them would be able to borrow again, from Mr. Mallikarjun or any other agent. The agents competed with one another when buying and selling produce, but they always shared information about loan defaulters.

Basix lent Mr. Mallikarjun the money at 21 per cent interest, and insisted that he should lend it to the farmers at no more than 24 per cent, or 2 per cent a month. This was no problem, since he wanted to use the loans as a way of securing loyal suppliers. He considered himself to be a commodity trader, and not a moneylender.

Ms. Hanumakka borrowed Rs. 3,000 from Mr. Mallikarjun. The interest cost was lower than she would otherwise have paid, and she was able to get all the money she wanted from one source, which saved a great deal of time. More importantly, perhaps, she soon found out that Basix would be willing to lend her money direct, rather than through the commission agent, if she showed herself to be a reliable borrower. She hopes to take a Rs. 5,000 crop loan direct from Basix the next season, and then to 'graduate' to a Rs. 20,000 loan for investment in irrigation equipment. This will mean that she will be able to take two crops from her land rather then one, which will make a very substantial difference to her family's income.

Cotton Seed Production

Basamma and her sons Verrangouda and Shankargouda farm eighteen acres in Meerapur Village in Raichur District; five acres of this are irrigated. They had been cultivating various crops such as sorghum, sunflower and groundnut, but they were enterprising farmers and they wanted to try new crops and methods of cultivation in order to earn more from their land. Capital was one problem, and the local branch of the State Bank of Hyderabad lent them Rs. 15,000 in 1995; this was useful but it was not enough to enable them to plant some of the more productive crops.

The Regional Oilseed Growers' Cooperative Union (ROGU) at Raichur is a union of farmers' societies whose objective is to benefit oilseed growers in the area. ROGU supplies quality seeds to its members and buys back the produce for processing in its 120 tons per day oil mill. ROGU dealt mainly with sunflower seed and groundnut, but it also wanted to identify more enterprising farmers who might cultivate cotton seed. This was far more remunerative than the other crops, but it also required more investment because of the requirement of high standards of purity and germination. An acre of sorghum needs Rs. 1,000, and sunflower needs Rs. 3,000; cotton seed requires an investment of Rs. 50,000 per acre. Nearly half of this, however, is spent on labour, which is needed for delicate tasks such as pollinating each flower by hand. It therefore creates a great deal of village employment.

Basamma and her two sons were very enthusiastic when the ROGU field staff suggested that they might take the risk of trying this new crop, but they did not have enough capital to finance it, and ROGU had no loan funds of its own. At about this time, Basix had started its operation in Raichur, and had already made an agreement with ROGU that it would provide loans for farmers who were members of its affiliated oilseed growers societies. ROGU asked Basix to finance Basamma and her sons as well, and after appraising the proposal, Basix agreed.

The family cultivated three acres of cotton seed. The borrowed Rs. 90,000 from Basix at an annual interest rate of 24 per cent, less 3 per cent for on-time repayment, and they invested a further Rs. 60,000 of their own. They made a great effort to ensure that their new venture was successful. ROGU provided technical advice to them at every stage, and Basix staff visited the farm regularly to provide encouragement.

In April 1997, Basamma, Veerangouda and Shankargouda harvested the crop. They delivered the seed to ROGU, and samples were sent for testing the purity and germination percentage. The results were favourable, and in June 1997 they received a cheque for Rs. 270,000. They immediately repaid the Basix loan, plus the 21 per cent net interest charge, and after paying all their costs, including interest, Basamma and her sons made a profit of Rs. 120,000 on the crop. They propose to take a further loan from Basix in the following year.

Stone Polishing

There are over 400 quarries and about 250 stone polishing businesses in Bethamcherla in Andhra Pradesh state, over 100 km from Raichur. They produce a range of polished stone slabs for the building and construction industry, and the growth of the industry has created a boom in the area. Transport contractors, equipment suppliers and repair shops, hotels and restaurants have sprung up, and there are also three bank branches and over fifty small private finance company offices in the area. The Andhra Pradesh State Financial Corporation (APSFC), a government development finance institution which specialises in loans to small and medium enterprises, has advanced a number of loans in the area and its Bethamcherla branch has the best recovery rate for the whole Corporation.

Mr. Raju worked in a number of stone polishing factories and he wanted to set up on his own. He went into partnership with Katha Anki Reddy, who shared the same ambition, and they bought a third of an acre of land for the purpose with their own money. They obtained all the necessary approvals for a slab polishing unit from the various government departments, and submitted an application to the APSFC for a term loan of Rs. 350,000; the partners were investing a further Rs. 130,000 from their own resources. Many months went by. The partners had to make repeated visits to the APSFC local office, and to the head office in Hyderabad, and there seemed to be no end to the delays. Other prospective borrowers told a similar story.

Basix had recently started operations. Its staff had recognised the need for finance in this industry, and they had called on Mr. Hussain Reddy, the President of the Slab Polishing Industries Association, three or four times, in order to promote their new approach to financial services. Mr. Reddy suggested to some of the newer members of the Association who were having difficulty raising finance for new units, such as Mr. Raju and Katha Anki Reddy, that they might consider applying for loans from Basix, even though its interest rate, at 21 per cent, was about 2 per cent more than APSFC. Apart from the promised fast service, Basix were also willing to include the cost of the electric power transformer in the project cost, which APFSC were not.

Raju and Katha Anki Reddy submitted applications to Basix, along with ten other members of the Association. After the papers had been appraised Basix approved five loans, including theirs. They received a loan for Rs. 350,000, out of the total project cost of Rs. 480,000, repayable over four years in monthly instalments, starting six months after disbursement. The plant was rapidly installed and started operations only four months after the loan had been sanctioned; Raju and Katha Anki Reddy made their first repayment immediately thereafter.

Within a few months the partners secured an order for a whole year's production from a contractor who was rebuilding houses which had been damaged in the earthquake in the nearby state of Maharashtra. Nineteen workers are employed, and the partners are pleased to be running a profitable and successful business of their own.

Basix Finance

Basix Finance, the institution from which all these people have borrowed money, was set up in Hyderabad in 1996. Its mission is to promote rural livelihoods, and to show that financial and related services can be provided to rural people in a way that is accessible and affordable for them and sustainable for the institution.

Basix attempts to do this by using a variety of different linkages, such as self-help groups, NGOs, commission agents and private companies, as well as by dealing direct with larger clients, when their business is sufficient to justify the expense.

The first branch of Basix opened for business in Raichur in June 1996. By 31 March 1997, after about ten months of operations, the financial position of the branch was approximately as follows (figures in rupees):

Assets		Liabilities	
Cash	1000	Owed to head office	1,577,000
Bank account	331,000	Interest payable	388,000
Deposit account	10,000,000	Bank overdraft	7,619,000
Interest owing	1,812,000	Borrower deposits	1,400,000
Rent etc. deposits	37,000	Long term loans	13,816,000
Advances	12,996,000	Surplus	600,000
Equipment	223,000		
Total	25,400,000	Total	25,400,000

The income and expenditure for the first nine months of operation, from June 6 1996 to March 31 1997, were approximately as follows:

Income		
Interest and service charges on loans		1,800,000
Interest from bank deposits		976,000
Total Income		2,776,000
Expenses		
Interest on borrower deposits	110,000	
Interest on borrowings	242,000	
Bank overdraft interest	537,000	
Salaries and allowances	643,000	
Professional charges	18,000	
Travel	448,000	
Other administration	178,000	
Loss provisions at		
4 per cent of portfolio	520,000	
Total Expenses	2,696,000	
Surplus		80,000

Because many of its loans were for short terms, the Basix management had decided to put the lump sum of ten million rupees on deposit with a local commercial bank, and then to borrow on the security of this amount as they needed. The high interest rate earned on the deposit more than covered the interest charged on their overdraft.

These figures give a reasonable view of the costs and revenues arising from the operations, but they do not give the complete picture, for a number of reasons. The costs include the salaries and other costs of the ten staff and three commission agents who are based in Raichur, but they omit most of the head office administrative and management expenditure, which amounted to 3.7 million rupees. Much of this expenditure was incurred for long-term business development, including planned operations in the States of Orissa and Bihar, and for funds acquisition and for securing a banking licence. These costs were in any case more than covered by grants from various sources.

The major source of loan capital during the period was an interest-free bridging loan from the Sir Ratan Tata Trust, which had been given to enable Basix to start operations while the final arrangements for long-term capital funding from the Ford Foundation and the Swiss Agency for Development and Cooperation were being completed. This means that the figure for the cost of funds is unrealistically low. The long-term capital funds will also be provided at artificially low interest rates, since they are intended to form the equity base on the basis of which it will be possible to borrow funds at commercial rates. It is planned that by the end of March 1998 these borrowings will already amount to almost 150 million rupees, but the business of the Raichur branch should by that time have expanded to a level where the interest costs can be covered.

The cases of the individual borrowers demonstrate that one novel feature of Basix is its willingness to extend very short-term loans, thus reflecting the financial needs of its clients, and enabling them to proceed rapidly to larger loans once they have established their credit worthiness with smaller amounts. The above figures thus do not reveal that Basix in fact disbursed a total of eighteen million rupees during the ten-month period, to almost 1,000 borrowers. The average loan was for Rs. 6,000, but some of these borrowers, such as the commission agents in Raichur market yard, on-lent their Basix loans to many smaller borrowers, so that the total number of ultimate 'beneficiaries' was almost three thousand.

About one-third of these borrowers were women, and almost 90 per cent of the money lent was for farming. Basix plans in 1997–98 to increase the proportion of loans going to women, and also to increase the share of loans going to non-farm rural enterprises. This is not only for social reasons, but because women are generally better payers than men, and because non-farm businesses are less subject to drought and other risks than farming. During the first year, ninety per cent of the loan instalments were paid by the due date. The main reason for the ten per cent of arrears was the bad weather which hit sunflower growers in some villages.

By the end of March 1998 Basix plans to have reached almost 15,000 borrowers, and to have a loan portfolio of 130 million rupees. By that date there should be four operating branches. The long-term plan projects that by its tenth year Basix will have a loan portfolio of 13.5 billion rupees, or almost 400 million dollars, and will have reached almost 400,000 borrowers. This would still represent only about one per cent of the rural poor of India. More importantly, therefore, it is hoped that Basix will also achieve its target of 55 per cent return on net worth by that time. This will show that lending to and for the rural poor need not be a money-losing activity.

(Note: This case was written with the help of Vijay Kulkarni, Unit Manager of Basix in Raichur, and Vijay Mahajan, Managing Director.)

Comments and Questions

Basix is not owned by its members, it is not a long-established bank which has 'discovered' micro-finance, nor is it an NGO which has moved from welfare or other activities into micro-finance. It is a 'new generation' financial institution, which has been set up to demonstrate that finance to promote rural livelihoods can be the basis of a profitable business. Basix aims to be profitable and to expand, but it also aims to be imitated, so that the benefits of whatever it achieves can be made available to far more people than it could itself ever hope to reach.

The sources of its capital reflect the fact that Basix' main goal is not to make profits for its owners. The investors expect eventually to recover their money, with a modest return, but they anticipate that Basix will be able to use their investment as the basis for raising the very large sums of commercial money that will be needed if its plans are to be realised. There will be profits if the business develops as expected, but they will have to be ploughed back into Basix, in order to increase the capital and raise further finance.

The case study describes the five different distribution channels that Basix is using in order to extend its outreach without losing money. The bangle traders and the potters are borrowing through self-help groups, similar to the Kalanjians in Madurai, and the groups which are being financed in Balipatna and Pingua in Orissa.

Basix is reaching the sunflower farmers by working with one of India's largest companies. ITC Agrotech has the finance which its growers need, but its management believe that they should concentrate their energies on their 'core business', oil milling, rather than being involved in peripheral services such as agricultural finance. They are therefore using Basix as their financial intermediary. Basix can be confident that its customers will receive good advice and will sell their crop for a good price, and all parties appear to have benefited from the arrangement.

Traditional commission agents provide another channel. In this case, they borrow funds from Basix which they then on-lend to small farmers. Basix deals with one large customer rather than many smaller ones, the commission agent can secure reliable supplies and the supply of credit to small farmers is increased. Again, every party should benefit.

The Regional Oilseed Growers Union is yet another facilitating intermediary. Here Basix lends directly to the farmers, but on the recommendation of the Union. This extends Basix' outreach, and, like the other channels, customers who borrow or are introduced through the intermediary may also in the future become direct customers of Basix when they have proved their credit-worthiness and are in need of more substantial sums.

Finally, some customers such as the stone polishers are borrowing direct from Basix, without any facilitating or financing intermediary. Their loans are large enough to justify the time spent on appraisal and supervision. These are fairly large borrowers, and their loans hardly qualify as 'micro-finance'; nevertheless, these customers are willing to pay 2 per cent more for their money in order to get the service they need. Access to finance is more important than its cost for them as well as for the bangle sellers, the potters and the farmers who are borrowing from Basix through other channels.

Questions

1) Basix is capitalised with subsidised money. What message does this convey to private profit-seeking investors who may be considering investing in micro-finance ?

2) Basix' investors, and its promoters (who have also invested their own money in it), need to be sure that the institution is achieving developmental goals and genuine additionality rather than using its low cost capital merely to offer lower cost or better service to clients who would have had no difficulty in raising finance from other sources. How can they do this, without unnecessarily complicating the task of the field staff ?

3) Does Basix run the risk of strengthening existing inequitable relationships by working with companies such as ITC Agrotech, or by financing clients such as the stone polishers? Should they seek more radical channels in the interest of promoting social change ?

4) Basix has lent through five fundamentally different types of channel, and its customers are spread over a wide geographical area. Is this too diverse, and should Basix not focus its energies on one type of channel, or in one small area ?

Section 3
CONCLUSIONS

CHAPTER 20

CONCLUSIONS

Micro-finance is a business, and micro-finance programmes which aim to assist the poor must be designed and managed in a business-like way. This is obvious, but it is also new. Many schemes which are intended to provide credit to the poor have been designed not as businesses but as welfare programmes; they may or may not be well-managed welfare programmes, but the whole basis of such programmes is different from the case studies in this book. The main conclusion, which is not original, is that micro finance institutions need to be managed like any other business.

The many manuals and guidelines which have been produced in the field therefore stress the importance of good management; financial products must be designed to address client's needs, they must be effectively marketed and distributed so that they reach the target market, prices must cover costs, records must be up-to-date and meaningful and management information systems must show staff at every level what is happening, staff training must be practical, funds must be mobilised as economically as possible, high rates of recovery must be maintained, and so on. These tasks are not easy, but they are not contentious either; everybody agrees that they must be done.

Good management is often no more than common sense, but common sense is far from common, and there is an enormous need for training in basic management skills of this kind, particularly for staff of NGOs who are quite unfamiliar with financial services, and for bankers who until recently have not been free to manage.

This book, however, is intended to pose questions to which there are no clear answers. It does not pretend to be a manual of best practices, of which there are many. Its aim is to promote diversity through debate and discussion rather than to impart specific skills.

We shall conclude, therefore, by restating some of the critical issues which have run through the case studies. The questions which follow are by no means an exhaustive list of the issues facing micro-finance institutions. There are no universal 'yes' or 'no' answers, but these and similar questions have to be faced, and answered, for every specific institution and programme. As is often the case in management, trying to find the right questions may be every bit as important as answering them, once they have been asked.

With the possible exceptions of Bangladesh and Indonesia, only a very small proportion of the potential customers for micro-finance actually have access to the kinds of service described in this book. Several of the cases show that informal moneylenders are not all extortionists and exploiters of the poor, but are offering reasonably-priced services which are complemented rather than replaced by formal micro-finance. Nevertheless, it is clear that there are millions of people who could presumably benefit from formal financial services in the same way as the numerous clients who are described in the case studies. The new approaches have only reached a small fraction of the market; micro-finance must be 'massified'. In business terms, the new products have been market-tested, but they now need to be mass-marketed.

Mass-produced products often have to be manufactured and marketed quite differently from their prototypes, and micro-finance is the same. Many of the questions which follow, therefore, relate to the task of scaling up or massifying micro-finance.

It is accepted that micro-finance is a business, and we shall therefore introduce the questions under the traditional management headings of marketing, finance, human resources and strategy.

Marketing, customer selection, products, prices and delivery:

> Should micro-finance institutions try to retain those of their customers whose enterprises grow and need larger loans and different services, or should they encourage such clients to 'graduate' to other institutions, such as the existing commercial banks, so that they can remain focussed on their core business, the microenterprises of the poor ?

It can be argued that the profits from dealing with larger clients can cross-subsidise less profitable services to others. As financial markets become more competitive, however, it will become more difficult to make high profits from any segment of the market, particularly for businesses which do not specialise. It may be possible today for organisations such as KREP and PRIDE to serve a wide range of clients, but in the long term it will probably become necessary to focus on one segment. If the aim was only to make profits, it might be advisable to 'trade up' with the more successful clients, and to abandon the original micro-finance market. As long as this market exists, however, institutions which have been set up for development rather than profit purposes must remain true to their origins.

Conclusions 179

> Women are more reliable borrowers and savers than men, and they use the profits of their businesses for their families rather than for themselves. Women's businesses tend to remain small, however, because their owners have other commitments; they do not grow and create jobs for others as successful men's businesses do. Most micro-finance institutions focus mainly on women, and they use various forms of group intermediation which are more acceptable for women than men. Most people, men and women, want to be employed, not to be self-employed. Is the current focus on women clients likely to delay the emergence of larger businesses which will create sustainable jobs for others?

The answer to this question may depend on one's view of the way in which the less-developed economies are likely to evolve. If they will become like the industrialised countries, where the majority of people are employed by others, and the self-employed are a minority, it may be reasonable to try to accelerate this process by 'picking winners', which are likely to be men, and assisting them to grow into large employers.

If the less-developed economies are likely to evolve quite differently, with far more self-employed people, or with many collective rather than individual-owned enterprises, the present focus may be the right one. A third view might be that the less developed countries will not change very much at all, so that micro-finance will be a self-sustaining form of poverty alleviation, rather than an instrument of growth. In that case, the focus on women is surely correct.

> Most of the programmes in these case studies are 'minimalist', in that they only provide financial services, possibly accompanied by group facilitation and simple training in the procedures demanded by the system. Do people need an integrated package of services, such as technical and simple business skills, access to new technologies and marketing assistance, or can they make profitable use of finance on its own?

As with all these questions, the only true answer is 'it depends'. The micro-finance movement is in some ways a reaction to the failure of services for small business such as bookkeeping training, which has made little difference to the trainees' businesses and for which they have very rarely been willing to pay cost-covering fees. Donors have enthusiastically welcomed financial services because they clearly benefit their clients and their costs can be covered rom client interest payments.

There is presently something of a counter-reaction. If someone borrows money for micro-enterprise which fails because the market is saturated, or because she lacks the necessary skills or technology, she loses her livelihood and her capital, and she still has to repay the loan. If too many clients are in this position, the institution which lent them money will also be in difficulties. Some of the most vigorous advocates of non-financial services are from institutions which are suffering because of the diversion of donor funds to micro-finance, and their concern is thus personal as well as professional.

The continued expansion of micro-finance is already leading in some places to market saturation in activities such as cereal trading and simple food processing, and clients who have succeeded with small loans may wish to expand into areas where they do need training and other non-financial assistance. The Grameen Bank in Bangladesh is promoting new forms of enterprise such as village telecommunications, but this is being done through a separately financed and managed institution. The Start-Up Fund in South Africa requires its clients to buy training and continuing counselling, but this is also part of the appraisal and supervision process, and is subcontracted to other organisations.

There is and will be a need for non-financial business development services, partly because of the success of micro-finance. They should however aim to be self-sustaining, and they should not be provided by the micro-finance institutions.

> Clients whose enterprises fail through no fault of their own may end up being worse-off than if they had never borrowed, and they are likely to be the most vulnerable. Is this a real problem, and how should micro-finance institutions try to address it ?

It is difficult to identify failures; the poorest people are generally the least visible, and people who are enjoying the benefits of belonging to a system are reluctant to point to others who have dropped out of it. Failures do occur, however; farming is risky, particularly when it is on a small scale, and poor people are the least able to afford the loss of their own capital, quite apart from having to repay a loan which has generated no income.

Some programmes, such as Grameen Bank Bangladesh and BRAC, include group emergency funds which members can use to pay off loans for their colleagues who have failed. Group members sometimes pay the debts of their less successful colleagues, and the lender may never be aware that this is happening, but this form of relief depends on the goodwill and the ability of the members of the same group. The Islamic partnership approach deals with the problem automatically, but this is the only formal way in which the owners of failed enterprises can be spared the burden of repayment. As in any form of venture capital, the profits from the successful businesses cover the losses of those that fail.

Larger groups like the Kalanjian Federation in Madurai can afford to offer life insurance, and cover against specific losses such as the death of livestock, or even crop failure, but further work is needed in this area. Poor people have shown that they need savings facilities as well as credit, but they also need insurance. Micro-finance institutions must offer a full range of financial services, just like the 'financial supermarkets' which now serve the rich.

> Micro-finance institutions have so far been able to charge almost whatever interest rates they wish, because the only competition is from informal moneylenders who lack any economies of scale, and who must often add a premium to their costs because their loan contracts are not enforceable at law. As competition increases, and as clients require bigger loans for longer terms, will interest rates be reduced, and if so how will the institutions be able to maintain their levels of service?

The operation statements in these case studies show that some of the institutions are already highly profitable, and could easily afford to reduce their interest rates. Others are at an early stage of development, and will soon earn high profits if their expansion plans are realised. Some others, however, have used their effective monopoly to absorb their inefficiency by charging high interest rates.

The market as a whole has barely been left untouched, but there are certain places, such as Machakos and other similar sized towns in Kenya and some parts of Bangladesh, where several micro-finance institutions are competing vigorously for the same clients. The less-efficient players must be allowed to fail, but their clients must also be protected from loss. This means that only very strong institutions can be allowed to take savings from their clients, and that they will have to be strictly monitored and supervised like any other deposit taking institution.

> Many institutions charge interest rates on a 'flat' basis, rather than on the declining balance, thus almost doubling the actual rate charged. Clients may not understand the difference, and are more interested in access to credit than its price. Nevertheless, are institutions not being dishonest, and their exploiting clients' ignorance and their need for money, when they understate interest rates in this way ?

Clients themselves are usually less concerned with the price of credit than politicians, regulators and bankers. Clients, and staff, also find it easier to calculate and to understand interest charges which are calculated on the total amount of the loan rather than on the declining balance. Many programmes would not be sustainable if they had to charge their stated rates only on the declining balance of loans. They argue that if they were to state the 'real' rates they are charging they would face damaging criticism from people whose goodwill is important.

There are however practical disadvantages. If repayment schedules change, flat rates have to be recalculated, and borrowers who choose frequent and regular repayment schedules are actually subsidising those who repay the whole loan at the end of its term. Institutions which choose the short term expedient of charging interest on a flat basis are probably storing up trouble for themselves in the future by effectively concealing the price of their loans, and they have a duty to educate their clients, and the general public. Informal moneylenders often mislead their clients as to the real cost of their services. The new micro-finance Institutions should not do the same.

> The most successful marketers of consumer goods such as toothpaste or soft drinks do not own their own distribution channels. They price their products so that wholesalers, retailers and hawkers find it worthwhile to make them available whenever and wherever people want them. Should micro-finance institutions not use a wider range of outlets, like the commission agents in Cuttack, but also including existing moneylenders, shopkeepers, or home-based 'financial counsellors' ?

Groups are used as intermediaries in most of the case studies, and NGOs such as DSS also play an important role. In general, however, micro-finance institutions have thus far not been very adventurous in their choice of outlets, for savings mobilisation or loans, and they have a great deal to learn from consumer finance and hire purchase companies, insurance brokers, chit fund operators, 'susu' collectors in West Africa and many others.

This will change, and it will be all the more necessary for micro-finance to be supervised by impartial and effective authorities, to protect savers and borrowers from unscrupulous institutions and intermediaries. This will cost money, and the institutions themselves, and through them their customers will ultimately have to pay for it through taxes or other levies. This will be another cost which will compel them to be more efficient and will accelerate the demise of those which cannot.

Finance: Savings, Sources and Uses of Finance

> Should the new micro-finance institutions be allowed to mobilise client savings, as a service to their clients and as a source of funds, or should they have to conform to the same or even more stringent regulations as the existing banks, in order to protect client's money?

Savings facilities are as important as credit, perhaps more so for the poorest clients, and micro-finance institutions need to mobilise deposits to complement and eventually to replace subsidised funds. Clients' savings must be protected, however; poor people cannot afford losses, but the reputation of micro-finance must also be preserved.

The new concepts are by no means universally accepted, particularly by traditional commercial bankers, and the whole movement could be threatened by a highly visible failure. Some institutions have already failed, but there has so far been no substantial loss of client savings. Strict regulations, rigourously enforced, may delay the growth of some institutions. This is a cheap price to may for the long-term strength of micro-finance.

> Some programmes compel their clients to make substantial savings before they borrow, and while they are repaying. Access to these savings may be difficult, or may even be impossible unless clients withdraw from the whole programme, and even then they may lose their interest entitlement. This may put clients' savings at risk, and it also enormously increases the effective interest rate on the loans, at least in cash flow terms. Should forced savings be limited to whatever minimum is needed to establish that the client is able to make regular payments out of income, so that clients can enjoy the full use of their own limited resources and not be made to pay to borrow their own money?

Financial markets for the poor are far from perfect, and there is little competition in most places. If clients are willing to pay high interest rates, or to be denied the use of their own money, this in itself does not necessarily indicate that the institution is making reasonable demands on them.

Commercial banks often offer their customers short-term loan facilities against the security of their own long-term deposits, but these customers voluntarily choose to borrow in this way. Some banks in India which lend to self-help groups demand that the groups deposit as much as half the amount of their loan with the bank, and do not allow any of it to be withdrawn until the loan is totally repaid. After the half-way point of the repayment schedule, therefore, these groups are effectively paying the bank in order to borrow back their own money. Subsidised interest rates may mean that the Bank is paying a higher rate of interest on the deposit than the group is paying for its loan, but this is not a tenable arrangement in the long-term.

Forced savings should be minimised, and the real cost of loans should not be inflated, whether by mis-statements of interest rates or by excessive or over-complex savings requirements.

> Loan repayment schedules in some programmes are rigidly standardised, and require borrowers to start repaying as soon as their loan is disbursed, and to clear the loan completely within a pre-determined period, irrespective of the household cash flows or the timing of the income from the asset for which the loan is used. This method is easy for staff and clients to calculate and understand, and it simplifies record keeping, but it also cause hardship. Should repayment schedules not always be fixed to accommodate household cash flows, even if this does cost more to administer ?

One rule of agricultural credit for small farmers used to be that loan repayments should at no time make borrowers worse off than they were before. If a client borrows money to buy an in-calf cow, and has to wait three months before the calf is born and the cow starts to produce milk, and she has to start repaying her loan the week after it is disbursed, she will clearly be worse off during those three months.

Group members may informally assist one-another to overcome this kind of difficulty, as they do in cases of business failure, but this does seem to be a case of favouring administrative convenience over client needs. Competition may in time lead to a more client-centred approach, and this problem does not generally arise in self-help groups, such as the clients of the Dhenkenal Gramya Bank. The groups borrow in bulk on medium- to long-term, and they then agree on the repayment terms for each loan, based on their knowledge of each member's circumstances. Some clients of PRIDE in Machakos are moving to KREP, because they prefer the flexibility of the self-help group system over the Grameen Bank system. Like some other aspects of the pioneer systems, this may be a feature which changes as competition increases and clients come to expect more flexible treatment.

> The 'new wave' of micro-finance is over twenty years old. Many different institutions have used grants and subsidised funds to design and prove a wide range of different systems, only some of which have been described in these case studies. Has it not now been convincingly shown that micro-finance does not need cheap money, and should the continuing flow of funds not stop, since it perpetuates the belief that micro-finance is not a 'real' business at all ?

Inventors and entrepreneurs are all too aware that financial support for their ideas only becomes readily available when it is no longer necessary. The initiators of micro-finance, however, were motivated not by the desire for profit but by their concern for the poor. The issue may therefore be not the precise timing of the withdrawal of subsidy, but whether it should ever be withdrawn at all. Is micro-finance a public service which will always need some subsidy, like health, transport or education, or is it a business like toothpaste, which is good for people but which nobody argues should be subsidised ?

The case studies suggest the latter; some of the institutions are making profits which would be the envy of any commercial investor. Some 'mainstream' financial institutions are looking at the possibility of investing in micro-finance. Thus far, however, they have only made token investments, usually under a 'social responsibility' or community relations budget rather than as part of their main business.

Subsidies can enable individual institutions to grow faster than they could from their accumulated profits, but they may discourage other institutions from entering the field at all. There will always be a demand for subsidy, so long as it is available. Donors may have to accept, however, that the best way to scale up the movement that they have helped to start may be to put themselves out of business and say 'no', particularly to the most promising applicants.

Human Resources, the Staff

> Many micro-finance institutions, such as BRAC or BRI, use commissions, bonuses or other performance-based incentive schemes for their staff. This is quite contrary to the culture of NGOs and public sector welfare organisations, and even the best designed incentive scheme will divert staff from social goals. Should micro-finance institutions not aim to employ staff who are committed to helping others rather than to increasing their own incomes ?

This question can be viewed as part of the larger question as to whether micro-finance is a business like any other. The search for efficiency and productivity, however, need not be inconsistent with the pursuit of social goals. If the system of client selection is properly designed and implemented the clients will all be those whom the programme is designed to benefit. These are also the most profitable clients; women are more reliable borrowers and more regular savers than men, and poorer people are also less able than the rich to 'pull strings' to avoid repayment.

Incentive schemes do not absolve management from the responsibility closely to monitor indicators or social as well as business performance. Performance-related payment can make well-managed institutions even more successful, but they will accelerate the downfall of institutions which are badly managed.

Policy and Institutional Issues

> If a product or service can be supplied at a price which is profitable for its providers and affordable for its buyers, experience worldwide suggests that it will be more likely to be made widely available efficiently and effectively if it is supplied by privately-owned businesses. Is micro-finance a service of that kind, and who should own the enterprises which provide it?

The case studies include institutions which are owned by governments, by cooperatives, by societies, trusts or other forms of NGO, and by their clients. None is owned by a private for-profit business. As in any field, one should expect a diverse pattern of ownership. It is nevertheless paradoxical that an activity which is widely recognised to be sustainable, meaning able to cover all its costs including the cost of capital, tends not to be undertaken by private investors.

Moneylenders are of course the major exception to this, and there are also a number of small private banks in West Africa, Indonesia and elsewhere which are beginning to enter the field. Why have private financial institutions been so slow to become involved, should they be expected to do so, and should they be welcomed if and when they do?

Governments, and the foreign donors which have supported them, have for many years created the impression that the poor are not bankable. The new enthusiasm for micro-finance has partly changed this, but the massive and well-publicised commitments of grants and subsidised finance for new institutions have also suggested that micro-finance is not yet a good business proposition, and, by implication, that the poor are indeed not bankable in a complete sense.

There is also still a widespread view in many countries, particularly in government and NGO circles, that the private sector must necessarily be exploitative rather than developmental. There are many examples of private businesses, including large foreign-owned ones, which have done more harm than good to their suppliers, their employees and their customers. There is no reason, however, why state-owned banks should play a major role in this new field when the public sector is retreating from so many others.

Group ownership is another option, but the weaknesses of cooperatives are well known. It is to be hoped that the Masoko Madogo Madogo, the Madurai Kalanjian groups, and the Cuttack Urban Cooperative Bank, can avoid the problems so often associated with ownership by members, as the Grameen Bank in Bangladesh seems so far to have done. If micro-finance really is a good business proposition, however, there is no reason why member-owned businesses should dominate it any more than they do other fields.

It is probable, therefore, that private sector banks and other private financial institutions will play an increasingly important role in the scaling up of micro-finance. The globalised international financial market place offers many other attractive opportunities, however. Private profit-seeking investors will only come into micro-finance on a large scale if their entry is generally accepted, and if the playing field is level. They will also need to be rigourously supervised, although perhaps no more so than institutions under any other form of ownership.

> Profit-seeking institutions are evaluated by reference to the growth in their profits and the return on their owners' investment. Welfare institutions are evaluated by reference to the quality and quantity of service they deliver to their beneficiaries. Micro-finance institutions are a hybrid, with profit and social goals; how should they be evaluated ?

One reason for the popularity of micro-finance is that it seems not to pose the same awkward problems of evaluation which are associated with other types of development assistance. The debates over cost-benefit analysis and cost effectiveness can be ignored, and all that is necessary is to see how far up the 'ladder of sustainability' the institution has reached. When the final step is attained, and the costs of funds, administration, loan losses and inflation have all been covered, the institution can cease to be a subsidised 'project' and becomes a self-sustaining business which is evaluated by its profits.

The reality is of course not so simple. Micro-finance institutions have been set up to achieve social goals on a continuing basis, and their sustainability and profits are only a means to this end. This may change in the future, as private for profit businesses enter the field, but the existing players have nearly all been capitalised with grants and subsidised funds. The expected return is not profit, which is easy to measure, but social welfare, which is far more complex.

One possibility is to calculate the amount of subsidy that an institution has received, and to relate this to the incremental benefit that its clients have obtained. This benefit can be equated to the profit that the donors were expecting. It is always difficult, however, to ascribe a given benefit to a particular input, such as financial services. Such studies are expensive to carry out, they distract the institution's staff and its clients from their work and the results are often contentious.

An alternative is to monitor simple quantitative indicators such as the numbers and amount of loans disbursed, the client profile and the rate of on-time recoveries. Basic data of this kind, together with figures for profitability, can be supplemented by occasional in-depth sample surveys which attempt to measure the impact on clients' household incomes, their possession of assets, their food consumption, their housing conditions, their health, their social position and so on. Subjective judgements will be necessary to decide on any trade-offs that may seem necessary, but there are no automatic answers, and any form of management involves personal judgement.

In the long term, however, competition should make it possible for customers to evaluate micro-financial services in the same way as they evaluate any other product they buy; they can 'vote with their feet', and buy elsewhere if they are dissatisfied with their present supplier. It will be many years before most people have a choice, since only a small proportion of the market is as yet reached even by one institution. The eventual aim, however, should be for micro-finance to be as widely available as any other consumer product. Decisions about funding, staffing, ownership and system should all be made towards this end. Micro-finance need not be treated as a 'human right', like education or clean water, because it does not need government or donors to pay for it. What it does need is institutional flexibility, good management and open minds; it is to be hoped that the examples in this book have shown what these qualities can achieve.